LIKE THE DAYS

of the

HEAVENS

above the

EARTH

AIDE PARRA

979-8-88540-615-4 (paperback)
979-8-88540-616-1 (digital)

Christian Faith Publishing
832 Park Avenue
Meadville, PA 16335
www.christianfaithpublishing.com

Printed in the United States of America

Based on a True Story

CONTENTS

1

CHAPTER

My Outer Body Experience

The day had finally arrived. It was March 30, 2015. I was twenty-nine years old, and I was forty weeks and one day pregnant. My name is Aidé Parra.

This was my first pregnancy, and I was anxious to meet my little baby boy. I was ready to get him out of my belly and see his little face.

You see, I had struggled with infertility due to a diagnosis of endometriosis. Let me take you back a little into my life.

I was married for the first time in 2006. I had not given myself to anyone before marriage; therefore, I was unaware that I would suffer with endometriosis. After a year, my marriage ended. Not planning on remarrying any time soon, I moved on with my life and moved to Waco, Texas. After all, I was only twenty-two years old.

Not long after moving to Waco, I met another young man named Carlos in a Hispanic dance club. Carlos was not much of a dancer, but there was something about him that I was drawn to. Later on, he became my boyfriend.

Let's fast-forward to the end of 2011. I met Isabel Miranda, a waitress in a very small Mexican restaurant in Riesel, Texas, where I worked as a high school teacher. I would go almost every morning to buy some breakfast tacos before going to work. She would talk to me about God and the Bible, and if I got my order to go, she would slip in written Bible verses in my bag. One day, I was at a very low point in my life, and my relationship with Carlos was off at that time, so I decided to ask Isabel for the location and time of the church she attended. The next service was until Sunday. I decided to go, and I

1

realized that I needed God in my life. The following week, I accepted Jesus Christ as my Lord and Savior. I was ready to live a new life in Christ and start everything anew. I was also ready to kick Carlos to the curb for good; however, he started to go with me to church.

My conversion happened very quickly and very boldly. I started to read the Bible, pray every day, and truthfully ask the Holy Spirit to dwell within me. I stopped listening to secular music, I didn't go back to the night clubs, and I stopped dressing with the miniskirts and a bunch of makeup. It was a drastic change. I knew it, and the devil knew it. I attended all church services from there on out.

This is where all my experiences started, so buckle up because I will take you on a ride. A ride that God Himself planned and destined for my life. A journey that I had perhaps for the purpose of writing this book. I hope this will be an encouragement for you to go out and trust God with everything you have.

Not more than a month after my conversion, I had a very vivid dream one day, where I saw the devil face-to-face. He couldn't get near me because I had a ring of fire around me that protected me. Then, he pointed to my boyfriend, Carlos, who appeared to the side. He said that maybe he couldn't do anything to me but that he was going to take Carlos. I saw an entrance to hell and people tied up in chains in single file line walking slowly into the entrance. These were people that were still alive but that were already headed to hell. Carlos was one of those in the line. He then told me that Carlos was his and there was nothing I could do about it. I turned to look at Carlos again who was now standing close to me, but he was not saying anything and seemed in a trance. He was unaware of anything happening around him. The ground started to shake, and a hole opened up underneath the ground. I ran to Carlos, and I was able to grab his arm before he fell down the hole. I was squatting over him using all my physical strength to keep him and myself from falling. Then the dream ended. That was a very strong dream, and I was a bit scared about what I would face in my walk with God, but I was comforted that I had a hedge of protection from God.

A few days later, I had another very lucid dream. I was lying in my bed, and I woke up because I knew that some evil spirit had come into my room. In my dream, I was lying in bed, and I lifted my head to see who it was. I saw it in front of my bed staring at me. Then the dream suddenly became real. I was aware of everything happening around me. He looked very much like the grim reaper. He was wearing a gray hooded robe and carrying a scythe. He stood still for a few seconds until I tried to stand up. He, or it, came on top of me and was trying to get into me. I had a physical fight with this spirit. The interesting thing about this is that I was only able to fight back with my left arm. Why one arm and not two? Or why not fight him off with my entire body? I don't know the answer to that. I just know that my left arm was the only thing keeping him off me. I used all my physical strength to push him off, and it worked. As soon as I had overcome it, the dream stopped. My arm was sore and hurting for about two days after that night. That is how I knew that it was more than a regular dream.

I told my life group leaders from church about what I was experiencing, and they told me to pray for those spirits to leave. I would pray every night before going to sleep and every morning as soon as I woke up. I asked God to always protect me.

Well, another few days later, I had a third experience. It was even more vivid than the last two combined. In my dream, I was lying in my bed, and I opened my eyes because I sensed a big and strong demon coming from about a mile away. I got up from my bed and stood in the front living room area, behind the front door of my apartment. A righteous anger started to build up inside of me because I sensed it was coming to attack me. I felt the power of God flowing through my body. I was not afraid of it. I wanted it to arrive so I could kick its butt. It was a big, monstrous one headed toward me. I could not see it, but I could sense it. It was coming fast at first; then, once I got up, it slowed down. I felt it when it arrived at the apartment complex. I started to speak words out loud directed to this spirit. I was not praying for God to protect me; I knew I already had His protection, and I knew it wasn't time for prayer. It was time for spiritual warfare. I started to say things like "you are not allowed to enter," "I cast you to hell in Jesus's name," "you have no power and no authority." "Jesus is my Lord and Savior, and you cannot harm me. Jesus is now the ruler here, not you. Jesus, Jesus, Jesus, Jesus." As I was saying these words, I felt power flowing through my body, and I was lifted up in the air as if I was flying. I wasn't just saying words; my words had power to them. I felt the demon directly outside my door; it had finally arrived. I was beginning to think that it wouldn't arrive anymore because it took so long to get there after it was coming so fast. I spoke to it again and said to it that it could not come in, not then, not ever. I once again said, "In Jesus's name, leave." The demon then left. I sensed it leave without it coming in my door. It left and never returned.

As soon as that fight was over, the power slowly left my body, and I walked back into my bedroom and back into my body. Three seconds later, I woke up remembering everything I had just "dreamed." I got up to get a glass of water, prayed for a little bit, and about two hours later, I went back to sleep. I was a bit shaken up by this for about two or three days afterward.

I guess I passed the test because God took it easy on me after that. I still had dreams, some were crazy and irrelevant, but others were not. I always knew which ones had a special touch from God.

Yes, that is how my Christian life started. Hopefully you haven't set this book down by now and called me crazy. I had not been taught how to defend myself against these attacks, yet I seemed to know what to do when it came time to act.

A couple months later, a few sisters from church asked Carlos and me if there was any impediment for us to get married, more particularly, if we were previously married and hadn't gotten a divorce. We both said no, so then they proceeded to tell us that living together was a sin and that we should get married. We told them that we didn't have the money for a wedding at the moment. They told us not to worry about the money, that the only money needed was the court money, which was less than $100. They got to work, and we started to plan a small wedding. The church had a big room for hosting small events in the back of the sanctuary. It was the church's kitchen and community area. My life group members volunteered to get something for the wedding. My sister paid for my wedding dress, some donated money to make the food, others cooked and served the food, while others made my wedding cake and decorated the place. The only major thing I had to pay for was the photographer. Thanks to my church life group and my family, Carlos and I had ourselves a wedding in April 2013.

Now married, Carlos and I were in right standing before the Lord. I grew in the knowledge of God and His word. My TV would almost always remain on a Christian channel.

I started to develop a stronger "hearing" from God. Sometimes they were thoughts that would come into my head, other times it was dreams, other times it was while reading the Bible, something would jump at me, if I can use that phrase.

I remember the first time I had a dream that was for someone else. In my dream, some woman, whom I did not recognize, told me that a sister in church was pregnant, and she was mentioned by name. I spoke back to this woman, saying, "I did not know this. This is such great news." In real life, this sister had not been able to get pregnant, and doctors were not giving her much hope.

I wrestled with the decision to say something to her or not because I was thinking what if it was just a silly dream and she is not pregnant, I would look stupid. But on the other side, what if this dream was given to me as a message to deliver to her that God had answered her prayers. I decided I'd rather take the chance of looking stupid if it turns out to be nothing than miss the opportunity that God has given me to be His instrument, if it turns out to be true. The only way to know if it was God or not was to test it. So I gathered some courage, and I went up to her and told her my dream. She said that she would check to see if she was pregnant. I didn't hear anything until a few days later. They announced in front of the entire congregation that she was pregnant. I was happy about her pregnancy, but I was more happy about the fact that it was God that had spoken to me. I cried, oh my goodness, I cried because God had used me. It was an amazing feeling.

From there on out, I yearned for God to use me. I would pray for God to speak to me in any way He wanted to so I could speak to others. In my heart, I wanted people to know that God was real and was present in our lives today and He wasn't a God stuck inside of a book.

Christian broadcasting really stirred this up in me when I would watch preachings or testimonials from people that God had used in this way. However, back in church, the belief was a little different. The people did believe in these giftings, but they believed that it was only for the "super spiritual," very consecrated, and everyone that God used this way didn't have a normal job; they lived of the gospel. Nevertheless, I kept pressing on and asking God to use me more and more.

Several months after that, another dream happened about a different sister-in-Christ. I dreamed that a giant snake rose up to destroy her, and she just stared at the snake and did nothing to defend herself. It turns out she was having marital problems and had separated from her husband at the time, which I did not about know before the dream. She and her husband did get back together. I was very happy that God would occasionally use me, and I'm glad it brought answered prayer to my brethren.

He would also answer my prayer for my family to be saved. One by one, my family members started to come to Christ after my conversion. It started with my sisters, then my brother, and finally, my parents became saved. It was truly a work of God. I had prayed long and hard for them to accept Jesus as their Lord and Savior.

However, I still had two unanswered prayers. I would constantly pray for God to give me a child and to take away my endometriosis. I remember one specific prayer during a church service. The prayer I made was "God, I'm trusting in you, but, Father, I want a baby before I turn thirty." I believe that approximately three months later, I got suspicious when my menstrual cycle didn't come down. I went to go get a pregnancy test, and to my surprise, it came back positive. I went to the same sisters that helped me with my wedding and gave them the news. I also texted my family in East Texas. My family told me to wait a little and take another one, and if that one was positive, then I could celebrate.

A few days later, Carlos and I went together to the medical clinic to get a more accurate test result, and sure enough, it came back positive. We drove to East Texas for the weekend to give my family the official news.

Jumping ahead to my pregnancy checkups, they were for the most part normal. The only problematic issue was my weight. I was losing quite a lot due to not being able to keep anything down in my stomach. I struggled the first four to five months with vomiting and constipation. I couldn't eat much because nothing would stay down. I lost about twenty pounds during the entire lapse of the pregnancy. At one point, I was starting to see my collar bones like when I was a skinny teenager. Over the months, I learned what foods would normally stay in my belly, although it was not always the case.

In August, I started my new job teaching at Bosqueville High School. I was hired during the summer before I became pregnant. Once classes started, I was not able to get up and go to work. Two weeks of instructional days had passed, and I had already been absent for a week. I knew I wasn't going to make it the entire year. I resigned during the third week of classes.

I used to vomit so much that I got used to carrying around throw-up bags everywhere I went. As a matter of fact, the day I went to the school to sign my resignation papers, I vomited in the parking lot before I went in; then, I almost threw up during the time I was in the office. Needless to say, they tried to get me out of there as soon as possible. Oh yeah, and I vomited as soon as I got back into the truck. That's just one day, I have a lot more of where that came from. Poor Carlos, I'm sure I made his stomach stronger during my pregnancy.

Weeks passed, and slowly I was able to keep food down more. I would get happy when I would step on the scale, during my checkups, and it said I had gained a pound or two. The only thing I dreaded were those appointments where they had to do a pelvic exam. I've always experienced cervical screening very painful. However, the baby was positioned where he should be, and everything seemed to run its course.

Sometime around the middle of my pregnancy, I had my ultrasound appointment. We found out the gender of the baby while I was getting the ultrasound. We were not wanting a gender reveal because we wanted to know the gender as soon as possible. Backstory, since I was a teenager, I wanted just two children. I wanted a boy first and a girl second. The ultrasound technician then announced to us that we were having a baby boy. We were very happy when she said that.

A few weeks after that, we were looking for a name in the big book of baby names. We wanted a name that sounded strong and masculine. We were trying to decide between two names, either Carlos Jr. or Adonaldo. Almost everyone wanted Carlos Jr., and although Carlos and I did like the idea, we knew people would end up calling him Junior. At the end of it all, we decided to name him Adonaldo. The big book of baby names said that the meaning of Adonaldo was "hope of God." We loved the meaning, and it had a strong masculine sound that we wanted. A few weeks later, my sisters from church threw me a baby shower. I got lots of presents. I knew this baby was a miracle, an answered prayer from God.

March came along, and I was now thirty-nine weeks pregnant, and the baby was not wanting to come out. I wanted the baby to be full-term, but I did not want to remain pregnant for more than forty weeks. My OB-GYN said we could keep waiting, or she could schedule an induction for the following week. I told her that I was not wanting to wait, so we set the date for March 30, 2015. That day, Carlos and I drove up at 7:00 a.m. to the hospital. I was telling him that we should stop to buy some breakfast burritos before we got to the hospital, but we were running late, so we skipped breakfast. I was more concentrated on getting to the hospital on time than on breakfast. We arrived at Baylor Scott & White Medical Center—Hillcrest. We registered and got in a room.

Everything was going smoothly. Nurses would come in and out to start prepping me with everything medically needed. Since I had a history of endometriosis and every pelvic exam was painful, my OB-GYN decided that she was going to give me some IV sedation before my labor induction. I was fully awake and aware of everything and was not able to walk around, but I was not in pain, thank God. I was healthy, I was never a smoker, I didn't drink alcohol, and I have never used drugs. I was not having any symptoms of fever, chills, chest pain, shortness of breath, cough, nausea, vomiting, or diarrhea. I was ready for the delivery.

I was initiated on oxytocin, and a few hours later, I underwent artificial rupture of membranes. Everything was going well. I had clear amniotic fluid, and I figured that it was only going to be a short time until the baby would be out. My mother, Lucia, is a registered nurse (RN) and had worked several years in a hospital delivering babies. So she spoke the nurses' language. I'm so grateful that she was able to be there with me; the nurses were also grateful.

Hours passed, and I was progressing appropriately in dilation. The only thing I was complaining about was the fact that I was hungry and I could not eat. When the nurses asked if I needed anything else, I would respond with "Can I get a cheeseburger, please?" They would of course laugh and say no but that I could have ice instead or they could give me a lollipop. I would say, "No thanks, that's not food."

More hours would pass by, and I was continuing to progress slowly. My mother would tell me stories about other women that would take up to two days, especially with their first baby. "The baby boys are the worst," she said. I tried to push that aside, and I would say to myself that it wasn't going to be my case.

I had passed the entire day without eating and, since around 9:00 a.m., without being able to get out of bed. It seemed like the hours passed by very slowly. My siblings had arrived at the hospital, and they would take turns going into my room to check up on me. We are a Hispanic family, so where one goes, we all go. However, there were only two or three people allowed in the room at a time, so the rest of them would all have to wait in the lobby area.

I still have a picture of my dad and the grandkids outside in a pond area with a description underneath saying, "Here just waiting on Adonaldo." They were all getting impatient. They had walked outside, inside, and had gone out to eat two times, and Adonaldo was still not coming out.

My sister Lilia, who is also a nurse, would go in to check up on me. She and my mother would talk in nurse language. So I would constantly ask, "Is that a good thing or a bad thing?" Everyone got a kick out of that.

The moment to start pushing finally came. I was fully dilated. It was some time after 10:00 p.m., and the nurses had brought in all the medical equipment needed for a vaginal birth. My plan was to deliver him without a cesarean. I was going to try as much as possible to deliver him as naturally as possible. I couldn't feel most of the contractions, so I had to rely on my mom, the nurses, or my sister that were looking at the monitor to tell me when it was time to push. My sister told me very excitedly, "You might just be the first to deliver a baby vaginally." The importance of her phrase was because my mother had my siblings and myself with C-sections, and my sister had her two kiddos with C-sections as well.

I pushed for about twenty minutes lying on my back with my buttocks just at the edge or just over the edge of the bed with my knees elevated. I kept hearing the nurse say, "I see his hair, he's coming." However, Adonaldo was not coming out.

They would get me to switch positions every ten to fifteen minutes. They even helped me get into a squatting position for another fifteen minutes or more. The nurse kept on saying, "The baby is coming, I see him." I don't know if she was telling the truth or giving me false hope. I did start to notice that little by little there were less nurses inside with me still helping me. At the end of that last position, it was mostly my mother and one nurse doing all the work. It seemed like the other nurses had given up on me.

Finally, after one hour of pushing, my OB-GYN walked into the room and evaluated me and the baby. She found my baby to be in the left occiput posterior (LOP) position. This is when the baby is facing forward and slightly to the left, looking toward the mother's right thigh. This increases the chance of a painful and prolonged delivery. She explained this situation to me, and she said we could still keep trying to have a vaginal delivery. To be honest, I wasn't understanding much of what she was saying because I was so exhausted. I was relying on my mother and my sister to help me decode her words. I was also making my family tired because by now it was almost midnight, and they had been helping me sit up and move.

At that point, I had to make some decisions. The doctor said I had another option, and that was the vacuum pump. During a vacuum-assisted vaginal delivery, a health care provider applies the vacuum—a soft or rigid cup with a handle and a vacuum pump—to the baby's head to help guide the baby out of the birth canal. My doctor did explain the risks to that option, and I decided against it. She said that she would let me keep trying a little longer and that maybe the baby could still rotate on his own.

They let me rest for about ten minutes and then got back to pushing. Another thirty minutes passed, and the baby monitor strip began to tell us that Adonaldo was beginning to struggle to breathe. The doctor's notes said, "There began to be recurrent variable decelerations." At times I believe God chose the wrong person for this because I'm not in the medical field nor in the science field, yet here I am. To explain this, I had to do some research.

According to Google, deceleration occurs when the baby's heart rate temporarily slows during labor. Variable decelerations happen when the baby's umbilical cord is temporarily compressed. Recurrent variable decelerations, where the decelerations occur with 50 percent or more of the contractions, are less common and more concerning. All of that to say the baby was not breathing right.

The doctor came in once again and said that I need to rest for twenty minutes. Everyone walked out of the room and left me lying on my side. They even turned the lights off in the room. I fell asleep for almost fifteen minutes of that time. I would wake up every five minutes or so, and I would check the time. I tried to stay awake, but I was too tired, and my body didn't have much strength left. After the twenty minutes of resting passed, everyone came back in the room, and I proceeded to push some more.

The only nurse that stuck around the entire time told me that I was tearing, and I was losing blood. I would push with all my strength when it came time to push, but now I couldn't push every time anymore. I had lost all my physical strength. The baby monitor told us that my baby was again struggling to breathe. That time, I really believed the baby had stopped breathing. Physically I was very weak, but mentally and spiritually, I was doing okay.

My doctor said that I had been in labor for two and a half hours and that by the looks of it, things were not going to change. She said that she had allowed me to try as much as she could but that to go any longer would result in the baby being in distress. Also, I had absolutely no more strength left in me to continue. I remained at peace and mentally positive. I said to my doctor, "You're the doctor, and you know what is best. God's will be done." I internally prayed for God to protect us. Overall, I was not worried about the next step. I knew that the decision was the correct one, and I didn't want to put my baby in danger. I remember telling God that if it was His will for me to die, then to just send Jesus to come get me and walk with me. I said that if He was going to take Adonaldo that I would understand. I might be a little mad at Him for a little while, but that I would come around. If He was to take us both, I asked for Him to just comfort Carlos. I had every possible outcome in my mind, and I was still at peace with whatever decision God wanted to make.

The doctor decided to proceed to a cesarean section, and I was in agreement with that decision. She began to review with me the risks of infection, bleeding (which could require transfusion and/or cesarean hysterectomy resulting in sterility), and injury to surrounding organs including but not limited to bladder, bowel, ureters, ovaries, fallopian tubes, nerves, and vessels. We discussed that injury could result in longer or additional surgery. We also reviewed possible injury to the baby. The NICU team was present to evaluate and care for the baby at the time of delivery. I of course couldn't go back to the house pregnant, so I proceeded. I signed all the necessary consents. I received one gram of Ancef in the IV and was placed under spinal anesthesia. I was told that only one person could go in with me to the operation room. I was uncertain if my mom or Carlos should go. I wanted Carlos to be there, but I could really use my mother's medical knowledge especially in that time of emergency. My mom convinced me that I would be fine and that Carlos, should be the one to go in with me. The doctor's notes continue on to say that I was prepped and draped in supine position, and I was then taken immediately to the operating room. Thank God for medical release records.

It was sometime after 1:00 a.m. by now. The feeling of not having any control of the outcome was starting to scare me for the first time. However, in my mind, I knew that God still had not left me and that God was the only one I could speak to at that time. My prayers at that moment were merely asking God to control my thoughts and to take control of the situation. I repeated that prayer many times during the trajectory to the operation room.

I remember seeing the big lights at the top when I arrived at the operation room; they seemed pretty to me. One of the first things they did as I got in the operation room was transfer me to another bed. I had a very strong sensation of falling off the bed as they were placing me in the bed. I weighed 172 pounds, and there were at least four of them lifting me. I expressed to them that if they let go of me that I was going to fall. They assured me that I was okay and that they would not let me fall. Carlos was not inside with me at that time. They had not allowed him to be inside with me until later.

I had been lying on my back now for several minutes, and this was causing me to feel as though I was suffocating. All through my pregnancy, I couldn't lie on my back, unless I was elevated because I would have difficulty breathing. I had to lie on my side.

After the switching of beds, I began to feel the sedation take effect on my body. I was not feeling any physical pain, although I could feel the tugging and movements of my body.

The anesthesia made its way up to my chest. This made my heart accelerate, and I felt it trying to jump out of my chest. I spoke to myself, in my mind, and I would command myself to calm down and to control my breathing. Psychologically, I was doing well. When I could not do anything else, I would use my mind to communicate with God. I knew that He was the only being that understood everything that was happening to me, everything I was physically feeling, and every emotion I was having. I was really struggling to breathe, and I wanted to ask how my heart rate was, but I couldn't. I also had this weird feeling that the bed was not entirely horizontal. I felt as if my legs were higher and my head was tilting downward. I could no longer feel or move my legs.

Then they told me they were going to give me oxygen and put the nasal cannula in my nose. This made me feel like I could not breathe even more, plus the oxygen was cold. I would beg the nurse to take it off because I couldn't breathe, but he would tell me that I needed it on. I would say to myself that maybe I was just feeling things and that I needed to relax. I asked God to be with me and not let me go.

I felt as if everything was being done so fast, and I couldn't keep up with everything happening around me. I had no idea how many people were in the room. I knew my doctor was in the room because I could hear her voice, but I didn't have full awareness of what was happening around me.

There were two things I was worried about besides my breathing and those were the losing of blood and the danger of the baby suffocating. I was worried the most for my son and if he was still breathing.

I thought, *This isn't right, this doesn't feel right.* I knew other women posted pictures, and they were awake and smiling during their cesarean sessions. It dawned on me that I was going through something that was out of the norm. I would start to worry, but then I'd bring it all back to God, and I would ask Him to take this from me. As I prayed, I had the feeling of just giving up on trying to figure out what was happening around me and just go to sleep. I was very tired, my body had no strength left, and I thought that sleeping through the entire procedure was best. My eyes at this point were closed; I was too tired to keep them open. The nurse next to me was asking me questions like "What is your name? How old are you? How do you spell your last name? Do you know where you are?" I would answer them, but after she began to ask me the same questions, I was beginning to get annoyed. It took a lot of effort to speak to her, and I was too tired to keep on answering the same questions. So I just stopped answering her. I heard my doctor say that she needed another doctor there to help her. At that time, I thought it was because I was in such a bad situation that she couldn't handle it on her own. I now know that it was standard procedure to get a second doctor, and it was not because she needed the help.

They finally let Carlos in, and I began to beg him to take out the oxygen. My eyes were still closed; occasionally, I would make the effort to open them and try to see him. I would also try to see the nurse or doctor that was trying to explain to me why I couldn't take off the oxygen. I would continue to beg him to take off the oxygen because I couldn't breathe with it. He finally took it off, doubting if he should. I would take deep breaths of normal air and try to calm myself down. Although it helped for about thirty seconds at most, I still continued to feel as if I was fainting. Carlos had to put the oxygen back on after about twenty seconds. I really wanted to lie on my side so I could control my breathing; however, that was not possible.

Carlos once again took the oxygen off, and I was able to take a few more deep breaths, but I was told to put the oxygen back on. In my head, I said, "Okay, I can't make this worse than it is, so in order to breathe right, I need to calm myself down and try to mentally overcome this. I must control my mind and my breathing." Then I prayed for my baby not to suffocate in my womb while he was being taken out. I had been in constant prayer since the day before, and prayer was the only thing I could do. I was completely relying on God to come out of this alive and with my baby.

Suddenly, I felt something that I'll try to communicate with words as much as possible. I felt a disconnection to this earth and to my body. I, or my soul or my spirit, was transported to what seemed to be outer space. I was looking at the dark space with its bright stars. I was not flying nor moving. I was merely contemplating the beautiful view and feeling the peace. This experience lasted for about twenty seconds. Then, as if in a blink of an eye, I was back on the operating bed.

The interesting thing during this time is that I could still hear some of the sounds around me even though I was contemplating the view of space. I was partially connected through my hearing but disconnected through sight.

In this place, I was finding myself at, I felt different and more relaxed. I knew this was something I had never experienced before. I was too weak to tell anyone, and even if I did, they would say that I was just imagining it. So I did the only thing I could do, I would speak to God, and I would say to Him, "Lord, if you want to take me, if that is your will, I accept it. Just come and get me to take me with you. If not, then please help me with this."

After that prayer, I one last time asked Carlos to please take out the oxygen so that I could breathe. He said no because the nurse didn't want him to. I then didn't fight to stay awake and aware anymore. I thought that sleeping would probably be best.

Then out of nowhere, once again, I was disconnected. Once again, I was seeing outer space and its beauty. I could still hear the sounds of the nurses and doctors talking to each other, although it was a bit more mumbled. This time, I was in outer space for about thirty to forty seconds. Overall, it was the same experience as the last time. After those seconds, I came back into my body.

I was uncertain about what was happening to me at this point. When I returned back to my body, I tried to brush it off as if I was just dreaming or my mind was tired and wandered off. But the feeling was all too real; it didn't feel like a dream, I thought. But two similar dreams one after the other? Another important information is that those experiences made me forget about my breathing problems and even my son. While I was "up there," all my troubles were gone. No worries, no pain, only peace was all I could sense. I have never felt a dream to be that realistic, and trust me, I do have very realistic dreams quite often. There was no natural way to describe what I was feeling. I knew that my separation had no human explanation. The sensation of peace lasted for a few seconds after I came back into my body. There was no forgetting what I had just gone through.

I was still lying in bed half conscious, half asleep. I was waiting to see my baby's face as they took him out. I had no idea if they had cut me open and the baby was taken out or if he was taken into the NICU. However, I was not at all worried. The minutes passed, and I kept on hoping that if I just endured a little longer that I would see my baby as they brought him to me, but that was not the case. Everything around me started to get less noisy. The mumbling noises were also quieting. *Maybe the people have walked out of the room*, I thought. *But why would they leave me alone? Where is Carlos?* I tried as hard as I could to open my very heavy eyes. I looked up, and my vision was a bit blurry, but I was able to see Carlos. I only had enough energy to keep my eyes open for two seconds. I did see another medical person there as well. So I rested a bit knowing that I had not been left alone. I asked God to tell me where my doctor was and why she wasn't giving me any updates on my son or on what they were doing to me. I wanted for this cloud of confusion and uncertainty to go away. I wanted to be awake and alert and have knowledge of what was happening. I didn't care if we were in an emergency state with my child; I just wanted to know what was happening. But I just didn't have the strength and was just too weak. My head felt heavy, my entire body felt heavy, my eyes could no longer open. My mind was almost gone too. The last thing I remember saying to God was "Father, your will be done."

As I was writing this book, I would ask Carlos questions I had never asked him before. For example, "After you were allowed inside the operation room, were you able to see me cut open?" He answered yes. I also asked him questions specifically regarding time. I asked him, "How long after you went in did they start cutting me open?" He said about ten to twenty minutes. I asked, "What was going on during those twenty minutes?"

He said, "Nothing really, you were lying in bed, and I think they were switching out your IV fluids." I then told him that I had been seeing videos of C-sections, and some only took about five minutes, and the kid was out.

"How long did mine take?" I asked.

He responded, "About thirty minutes."

I was shocked. "Really that long?" I asked.

"Yes, they were really struggling to get him out. He was far down, and the baby was big," he responded.

But let's get back to my story line. I'd like to say that something finally knocked me out, maybe the anesthesia, maybe the oxygen, maybe God, maybe my body finally just gave up. In a moment, I found myself in space again for the third time. This time, I was not connected to my body here on earth. I could no longer hear the sounds coming from the operating room. I was in this "place," and I had no connection to anything here on earth. I was not thinking that I had died. I was not thinking that I had been taken out of earth. I was not even sure of my purpose for being "there." I was merely there. I had a body, but it wasn't entirely like my earthly body. I was about the same height and perhaps about the same body shape. I had no mirror, so I couldn't see my face or what I looked like. I was apathetic about how I looked, truthfully. There, my physical appearance was of no importance.

I was a being, not entirely human, not entirely spirit. I was wearing a white dress that came down midway between my knees and my ankles. I couldn't feel anything underneath my feet. I want to say that I had no sensitivity in my feet or I might not have had any feet. As strange as that sounds, I can't remember feeling the difference between stepping in air or stepping on floors.

I wasn't conscious about breathing; I had no breathing problems there. I had no hunger. I couldn't feel the temperature. I didn't know if it was hot or cold. I had lost my earthly memory, but I wasn't aware that I had lost my memory.

The Bible says that in heaven Christ "will transform our lowly bodies so that they will be like his glorious body" (Philippians 3:21). Maybe this is what I witnessed, although I can't guarantee it. Stay with me. I know some things are going to sound very strange, but I will try my best to communicate them to you as simply and truthfully as I can.

I noticed that I was no longer floating in air, but I was standing on something that looked like a concrete passageway. It was about three feet wide by ten inches thick. I couldn't see where it started or where it ended; also, it had no walls. It appeared floating in air or space; nothing was sustaining it from underneath. If I would have stepped out of it, I might have fallen off, but my mind didn't even contemplate the idea. It seemed like I was on a mission to get somewhere, but I was unsure where that somewhere was. As I walked on this passageway, more things started to appear before me. I could now see a door that stood on its own on the passageway. Following the door were many stairways going in different directions. All of which had no walls.

I'd like to call this area "the first floor." This area had a few walls although not all areas had walls. To give light, there were torches placed on the few walls that were *viewable*. I say viewable because some places had walls, but they were transparent, not like the plexiglass where you can see the glass, but it was a type of transparent that you definitely didn't know the wall was there unless you had prior knowledge of it being there. I could continue to see the outer space on the other side. There were some rooms on this first floor, but they were not fully enclosed rooms. The walls on these rooms looked like medieval architecture. The walls were made of stone cut into big squares, very much like a medieval castle would look over a thousand years ago. The torches were made of wood and fire, but the fire did not consume the wood. I tried to find the way on my own. I would go up a stairway, and I discovered that it led too far to the side, and I didn't want to risk getting lost, so I would return back instead. Eventually I did advance a little further up. When I reached the second level, I realized the stairs did not follow the laws of physics that we have here on earth. It was a nongravitational field, but at the same time, I was being pulled down.

Let me try to explain. The stairs I was walking on, some were right side up, and you would walk over them upright. However, sometimes the stairs would be upside down and in many different directions, and people would still walk on them. On earth, a person cannot walk upside down on stairs without falling on their heads. Yet in this other-dimensional world, there was no falling off. Also, the hair would not hang upside down like here on earth. This is the part that is the hardest to explain.

Just like how ants, here on earth, can walk on anything and in any direction. Ants are able to do this because they have tiny, hooked claws at the ends of their feet, which help them walk on the undersides of leaves and limbs. I walked in space similar to ants but without any hooks to cling to features of the surface.

I myself was never upside down because I never took those stairways. For the first five to ten minutes, I was just seeing all possible passageways or stairs I could go but without risking getting lost. On the first floor, I saw other people. I saw one man in particular that seemed very lost. He seemed like he had been wondering for a while. I also saw about five more people walking on different stairways. None seemed to acknowledge each other, although we could see each other. I didn't speak to anyone, and nobody spoke to me. I can't remember their exact clothing, but I can remember that their clothes were not entirely white like mine. I kept on walking on more hallways and stairways. In this area, I had a conscious knowledge of where earth and hell were located, but I could not turn to look at them. I knew earth was located some distance between fifty thousand and one hundred thousand miles behind me. I knew that people on earth did not know of the existence of this place because they couldn't see it. We knew of earth's existence, but earth or the people of earth didn't know of the existence of this place. Earth was another thing that was unimportant, just like my physical appearance.

There really is a separation between this place and earth, even though we were somewhat close. I find reference to this in the Bible in Luke 16:26, "And besides all this, between us and you a great chasm has been set in place, so that those who want to go from here to you cannot, nor can anyone cross over from there to us." In the New King James Version, it says, "There is a great gulf fixed." In this verse, Jesus was speaking about the rich man and Lazarus. Interestingly, this passage is about the rich man going to hell and Lazarus to heaven. I don't mean to stir up the debate of whether this is a parable or not, but this might just prove that Jesus's words were spot-on. But let me keep going with my story and let the theologians keep battling this one out.

About ten minutes later, I believe I "prayed" to God for direction. However, my prayer was very peculiar. It was not spoken with my mouth nor did I say it in my mind. I "prayed" to God from deep inside my stomach or chest area. My cry to the Lord came from within me.

I did not have very many times where I felt human emotions, two or three tops. Even when I had them, they were very weak and almost nonexistent. I wasn't panicking, I was in complete peace, but I didn't want to wonder like the rest of the people. This "feeling" only happened once, and it only lasted for about ten seconds. The answer came very quickly. I saw something flying, appearing and disappearing, above my head in front of me. The size of this was about eight inches in height by eight inches in length. It's hard to describe the width because it would shape into different things. At times, it would be flat; other times, it would shape into something thicker. It was something that only I could see. For now, let me call it my guide. At times, it would hover over walls; at other times, it would just hover in midspace. But my guide would tell me which direction I needed to take. If I made a turn somewhere, I would look around to see if my guide would pop up. If it didn't, then I knew that I had taken the wrong turn. Like I said, it would appear and disappear when it wanted to, but it never led me in the wrong direction.

In those fifteen minutes, I had climbed many stairs, and I had walked on many passageways. I had gotten to another floor level. I'm not sure if I would be on floor level three or level four since the "floors" are not like our conventional floors.

The man I was speaking to you about earlier, who seemed to be getting desperate, started walking out of desperation. He would go everywhere, but his disorientation was leading him down. This was the last time I saw other people.

I had gotten accustomed to following my guide. I would walk with more confidence since my guide was directing me. I got faster at turning corners and at walking up stairs. At this level, there were no more walls and no more torches, but it was not dark. The more I went up, the less stairways I saw. Until I arrived at the fifth floor, I'm going to call this floor level five for the purpose of this book. I now saw more open spaces due to not having as many stairways. I would stop and contemplate the beauty of space, but only for a few seconds.

I no longer saw my guide after this because I knew I had arrived at a very important place; therefore, its job was complete. I got to an area where I was standing on a square floor made of some form of concrete or stone. The size of this would be about six feet by six feet and about ten inches in thickness. I stood on this floor, and I looked out to space. The view was breathtaking. There were only two stairways from here; one was to the left, and it went up, and the other was to the right, and it went up for a few stairs, but then it went down.

Although my guide was no longer with me, I knew that to the left was the right way to go.

As I was about to step on the stairs to go up, I was stopped by God's voice. I immediately knew it was Him, and I was not shocked to hear Him. Again, human emotion was almost nonexistent there. His voice seemed familiar to me. I did not ask Him why He did not speak to me earlier. Hearing God there was much like hearing your thoughts but louder and clearer. All "hearing" came through my mind and not my ears. *Telepathy* would probably be the closest word I can get to describing it, although it doesn't entirely do it justice. I never saw God (nor Jesus) with my eyes, but I knew He was close to me. He told me to look out into the open space. I turned my body to my right so I could see it in front instead of turning my head. Then before my eyes appeared ropes with knots. It's crazy, I know, but this is what happened. These ropes looked like sixteen-inch hawser ropes in tan color that were extended out. Hawser is a nautical term for a thick cable or rope used in mooring or towing a ship. God didn't use the word *hawser*; I'm using it now to try to describe how they looked. There were about eight of these ropes all the same size and color. Each rope had a different number of knots that were knotted with the same rope. Let me put it this way, think of a knotted climbing rope. Climbing ropes are hanging vertically and have knots every eighteen inches, let's say. Well, the ropes I saw were similar to that except these ropes were placed horizontally versus vertically. I was not allowed to see the entire length of the ropes. I was only permitted to see a section of about ten feet in length. I was not allowed to see the beginning or the ending of the ropes.

God said to me, "Do you see the ropes?" I paused and looked at the ropes again. There was a distance of one foot between each of them. Nothing was holding them in place, and nothing was separating them, yet they were perfectly straight and aligned. I saw two of them in particular.

Then I responded, "Yes, I see them."

He then said to me, "Do you see the knots on the ropes?" Once again, I paused and observed the knots. Not all knots looked the same, some looked like stopper knots, others looked like regular overhead knots. One rope had several knots, let's say one or two knots every foot. While another rope had one or two knots in the entire ten feet length. The other ropes had different numbers of knots. No rope was similar.

After I noticed this, I responded, "Yes, I see them."

The rest of this conversation with God is the entire reason why I believe I was sent to this "place." God then spoke something that I had never heard before. He said, "You see each rope represents the trajectory of a person's life, their destiny. Each knot represents a trag-edy like a death of a family member or something that is going to mark this person's life in a sad, grieving way. I know this will happen. Nothing takes me by surprise. I made their destiny, I created it, and I know everything that has passed and that is to come. But I want you to tell them that even though they will go through these griefs, I will be with them. And those that go through the most tragedies, I will be with the most."

He stopped speaking, and the ropes disappeared. Things went back to how everything was before God started speaking. I knew God had stopped speaking even though He never said that He was done. I didn't have any follow-up questions. I seemed to understand every word He said. This is why I say telepathy doesn't do it justice because I had knowledge that was not "communicated" to me, yet I knew.

The language we spoke was not in any language that we have here on earth, none that I know of at least. Also, He didn't introduce Himself to me; He knew that I already knew Him.

With God not speaking anymore, I continued my journey up the stairway I was headed on before. I went up those last twenty steps approximately. I came into a hallway. I had not seen a hallway during this entire time. This area had a floor, walls, and a tall ceiling that were different tones of white and gray in color. It seemed to be made of granite with quartz grains that sparkled with the light, kind of like the granite countertops we see in homes or in stores, but instead of countertops, it was the floor, walls, and ceiling.

Let me say a little sidenote here. In the book of Revelation 21, John describes the New Jerusalem "coming down out of heaven from God" (verse 10). Then, in verse 11, it says, "Having the glory of

God, its radiance like a most rare jewel, like a jasper, clear as crystal." This is very much like the material I witnessed. I did take a geology course in college, but I barely passed it. So please forgive me if I don't know exactly what material I was looking at. Maybe John didn't know either, and he just described it the best way he knew how. After all, what jasper that we have here on earth can turn "clear"? I'll let you decide that on your own.

Let me keep going with my story. At the end of the hallway was the end of the path. There was a bright light radiating at the end of the hallway. However, this light did not come from the sun. It was another type of light. It was its own light source and perhaps energy source. It was very bright, but at the same time, it wasn't blinding. It gave just the right amount of light. I walked into this hallway, and the ceiling was about twelve feet tall, or maybe a little taller. The width of the hallway was a little tricky to tell exactly because I knew there were areas that were transparent, and I was not allowed to see, but I would guess that the width of the hallway was about ten feet. I knew there were other rooms on the other side of the wall with doors, but the doors would reshape or become transparent, so I could only see the straight hallway. Think of this like a hotel hallway with rooms on each side of the hall. I knew there were rooms on each side, although I could not see them. I slowly walked into this hallway. I felt very much alive here. On earth, we feel weighed down by the weight of our own body due to gravity, but up there, that weight was nonexistent.

I walked about three-fourths of the way to the end of the hallway; then, I knew that to the left was my room. A door appeared before me. I can't explain how I knew, I just did. I knew this was going to be my "resting place." Here I was going to be able to rest or, better said, sleep until the end of times or until God awakened me. This wait had something to do with Jesus's return. After this waiting time, I would be awakened to live again.

I touched the round doorknob to start to turn it. This was the only time I used the touch sense. This doorknob looked similar to the ones we have here on earth. I turned the knob and started to slightly open the door. As I did that, God spoke to me again. He said,

"Stop. You can't go in. You must go back." I let go of the door and took a step back. Sadly, I didn't get to see any part of the inside of the room. As I stepped back, I felt for the first time a human emotion. I felt very confused. I thought, *Go back to where?* I couldn't understand where I was going back to.

God said to me, "Remember who you are." As He said those words, memory started downloading into my mind of who I was here on earth. I started to remember things like my name and what I looked like on earth.

God spoke again and said, "Remember that you were pregnant." I remembered that I had a pregnant belly. Every time He said the word *remember*, it resounded in my mind and unlocked memory that was stored away somewhere. Memories started to come back to me. I still remained without saying a word, but in my confusion, I was wanting to fabricate a question, but I never had enough time to fully create the question.

The place I had been was starting to dissolve and disappear. I wasn't standing on beautiful white quartz floors anymore. I was falling back to earth but without the feeling of falling.

God spoke to me a third and last time. He said, "Remember you had gone to the hospital to give birth to your son…" While He was still saying those words, I felt my spirit or my soul back in the earth's atmosphere. I looked down, and I was about one hundred feet above the hospital roof. I had remembered just about everything about my life. "But don't worry. Your son has now been born." As He said that, my spirit or soul came back in my body. He then stopped talking again.

Three seconds later, I opened my eyes, and I was back in my body. I turned toward Carlos, and I saw his face for about three seconds. I realized that the time I had been away from earth was a few seconds, but I had been "up there" for about forty minutes or more. Time dilation? Perhaps, but time was not equal. After this, I closed my eyes and fell asleep. That was the end of that experience.

2
CHAPTER

Adonaldo Is Born

I am not a doctor, nurse, nor do I have any kind of medical degree. This information came directly from my medical records after I requested them, for the purpose of writing this book.

I reached out to my OB-GYN to get her input for this book; however, she didn't respond before I got done writing this book. Maybe she was busy, as all doctors are, and will eventually get back to me.

My doctor's notes say the following:

> An incision was made using a 10 blade scalpel in lower transverse fashion approximately 3 cm above the symphysis pubis and was carried down to the fascial layer. Fascia was entered sharply using a scalpel and extended bilaterally with Mayo scissors. Kocher clamp x 2 was used to grasp the anterior aspect of the fascia and the underlying rectus muscles were separated away both bluntly then sharply using Mayo scissors. This was repeated inferiorly in identical fashion.
>
> Rectus muscles were then separated bluntly, and the peritoneum was identified and entered bluntly. Stretching occurred to create adequate space. Bladder blade was placed. A bladder flap was created using a scalpel and extended bilaterally bluntly.

The infant's head was then elevated to the level of the hysterotomy after some struggle releasing vacuum in the pelvis and assistance of a vaginal hand was required. With failed attempts, a T was cut into the active segment and evaluation to attempt to deliver breech. This was not readily possible and attention was again turned to deliver the head with assistance of the vaginal hand, until the fetal head could be gently elevated to hysterotomy. Delivered with the assistance of fundal pressure. Infant was bulb suctioned, cord was clamped x 2 and the infant was handed to the awaiting pediatric team. Cord blood was obtained. Gentle traction was placed on the cord to deliver an intact placenta. 20 units of oxytocin were placed in her litter of lactated ringers and began running wide open.

Uterus was exteriorized from the abdomen and wrapped in a wet lap sponge. Dry lap was used to clear the uterus of clot and debris. Bilateral extensions were noted right greater than left. These were repaired following the initial repair of the T upward, then hysterotomy was closed using 0-Vicryl on CT-1 in running locking fashion and good hemostasis was achieved. Posterior cul-de-sac was cleared of all clot and debris. Normal appearing fallopian tubes and ovaries were noted bilaterally.

Uterus was returned to its anatomical position within the pelvis. Bilateral paracolic gutters were cleared of all clot and debris. Hysterotomy was then revised and found to remain hemostatic."

Hemostasis was achieved throughout the remainder of the abdomen using bovie cautery. Fascial layer was closed with 0-Vicryl on CT-1 in simple running fashion and good hemostasis was achieved. Subcuticular layer was closed using 4-0 monocryl on PS-2.

Patient tolerated the procedure well. All instrument, needle and sponge counts were correct x 2."

This patient should not attempt VBAC as active segment was involved with Hysterotomy.

Yes, this part was all capitalized on my doctor's notes.

This was electronically signed at 3:39 a.m. on March 31, 2015. This is what was happening to my body as I layed on the operating bed.

I don't have much information about the condition of my baby during the time I was knocked out. However, Adonaldo was not sent to the NICU, so I want to say that God did guard him from harm.

Around three o'clock in the morning, I started to slowly wake up. My eyes were for the most part closed, but for a few seconds, I would open them to see where I was at. I realized I was not in the operating room anymore. I would open my eyes and see nurses walking by. I tried to speak to them, but I could barely talk. "Where am I?" I asked a nurse that was walking by. She responded that I was in the recovery room. I asked if everything was all right with me. She responded that I seemed to be recuperating well.

That would use up all my energy, and I would fall asleep. Minutes later, I would open my eyes and attempt to talk to the nurses once again. I would ask them different questions, and I would ask them for my son. I would stay awake long enough to hear their short responses. I desperately wanted to get well and walk again. I wanted to see and hold my son. I figured that he was being taken care of by the medical staff, but I wanted to make sure of that. But how could I care for my baby if I didn't have enough energy to keep my eyes open, let alone walk?

Turns out that my family had stayed in the lobby area waiting to see how I recovered. The kids did go back home with my sister Natalia to sleep. I woke up, and my sister Lilia and Carlos, were there by my side. I can't remember if they woke me up or if I woke up while they were there. They asked me how I was doing and how I felt. I can't remember answering those questions, but I do remember telling them that I had been taken out of my body and on to another place. They probably thought I was still under the effects of the anesthesia or something. I don't blame them; my speech was probably mumbled, and I probably sounded drunk. They would tell me to rest and not worry about that at the moment. When I was telling them this, my eyes were closed because I used all my strength to speak.

While my sister and Carlos were still in the room, a nurse came by and pressed on my belly. That was very painful. I don't think I have felt that much pain in my life. I think I almost screamed out of pain, and if I didn't scream, I sure wanted to. The nurses have to massage your uterus to help it contract down. I'm not sure if the fact that I had my uterus taken out and then put back in had any effect on the amount of pain I was feeling, but it was very painful. It felt more like torture than a massage. After that beating, I again ran out of strength and fell asleep, so I was unable to continue to tell Carlos and my sister about my experience.

I was told later by Carlos that my parents went into the recovery room to check on me as well, but I didn't wake up to see them. That was the last I remember from being in the recovery room. A member of my family took a picture of me asleep in the recovery room, and it was 4:33 a.m. when they took it. I opened my eyes when they were moving me out of the recovery room into my normal hospital room, but I didn't have the strength to stay awake.

My family members went to see Adonaldo in the nursery. My father did say that Adonaldo was not doing well at one point but that they were able to stabilize him in the nursery. I'm not sure exactly what happened, but he was fine afterward. My family took pictures of him while I was recovering.

I saw Adonaldo for the first time at six that morning. I have a picture of that moment. I was too weak to hold my head up, so my father helped me lift my head by lifting my pillow under my head, and Carlos was holding Adonaldo close to me so I could see him. I saw him for a very short time because I was too weak, and I wanted to rest. I wanted to keep him next to me, so they laid him next to me and put him on top of my arm. I started to fall asleep, so they took him away so I wouldn't drop him or crush him. I felt them taking him away, and I told them that I still wanted to hold him. So they left him there for a little longer until I was fully asleep. I have a picture of me fully asleep with Adonaldo, who was also asleep, in between my side and my arm. I didn't want anyone to take him from me. I just wanted to hold him and keep him. After all I went through, having him in my arms made it all worth it and gave my mind peace, and I finally felt like I could rest. I'm sure they put him back in the hospital bassinet soon after I was fully asleep. In the pictures, I looked very tired, my eyes were swollen, and my face was pale. I thanked God for my baby being next to me.

Around 7:00 a.m., I had my first visitor in my room. It was my sister-in-Christ, Hortensia, who had come to visit me and see my baby. I remember slightly opening my eyes to see her and greet her. I still couldn't stay awake and alert for long, but I do remember having small talk with her. Simple phrases like "I am doing okay," "I am recuperating," I would say to her in Spanish. I believe my mother was in the room with me.

After the small talk, I proceeded to tell her my experience. I knew her well, and I knew that I could trust her with this information. So I began to tell her what I saw. I told her about the ropes and the knots and what God told me; it was a very summarized version of course. I was still with my eyes closed and not fully aware of my surroundings and still wanting to fall back asleep. She said that she had to go to work and that she would swing by later or another day, so we said goodbye, and I went back to sleep for a few more hours.

Once I woke up, the rest of the day went by more normally. I was able to stay awake and aware for several minutes or even up to an hour. I remember once I was fully awake asking Carlos for a big cheeseburger. My mom, being a nurse, said that it was a bad idea to eat that because it would be painful when it came time to go to the bathroom. I said that if I couldn't have a big burger to at least have a Subway sandwich. She still said it was basically the same thing, so I had to lower it down to a broccoli cheddar soup from Subway. I sent Carlos to go get me something because I was starving.

I ate slowly, but not long after, I was hungry again; this meant that I was getting back to my normal self. I could still remember everything that happened to me very vividly. I mostly kept it to myself because, well, it was a very "weird" experience. Normally, people that have gone to heaven have seen a beautiful place with many colors and living waters. Or on the other side, they have experienced the ugliness of hell. My experience was neither of those, but I knew it was real. But for the time being, I was focused on recuperating my body and my energy.

Every time I would look at Adonaldo, I would thank God for him and for allowing me to continue to live. Sometime in the afternoon, I started to get visitors wanting to see me and my baby. I was awake when they visited me, but I still felt very tired and in need of more sleep. I wanted God to explain to me what all happened while I was in His presence. "What was that place?" sometimes I would ask in my mind, but I wasn't really looking for answers right at that time; it was more curiosity than actual wanting to discover what place that was.

Once all visitors had left around nine or ten at night, all my family left as well except for my mother. She stayed behind to keep an eye on me at night. We were all very tired and in much need of rest. Everyone had held my baby longer than I had held him for, and I just wanted to keep him next to me at night. My mom said that we should send him to the nursery for us to rest. I had slept more than her, so I understood that she needed to rest, so I accepted to take the baby to the nursery. About 2:00 a.m., I woke up, and I felt like I needed to know how my baby was doing. My mother was asleep, and I didn't want to wake her up, so I tried to go back to sleep. About another hour, I woke up and decided to go look for Adonaldo. I quietly got up and walked to the nursery and tried to see if I could see him at least for a little while. However, I didn't see him, and I went back to bed. About another two hours later, I walked up to the nursery window and tried to see him once again, but still nothing. *I really want my baby*, I thought, but I knew that my mother had to rest, so

I went once again back to bed. This time, I stayed asleep until 7:00 a.m. I started to receive visitors in the morning again, and Adonaldo was brought back into the room. I was progressing on my healing, and Adonaldo was doing very well.

The following day, I received more visits from more family and friends, and my doctor visited me as well. Finally, on April 2, I was told that I was going to be released. I took a shower, got dressed, and was released from the hospital at three in the afternoon. I was in the hospital for three and a half days. And from there, I went to stay at my parents' house in East Texas for about a month until I was fully recovered.

I would remain in communication with "Father" as I like to call God. My connection with Him became more real to me. At times, I wondered if I would ever see life or earth the same again. I knew that after that experience, God was more real to me than ever before. I was unafraid of death because I knew that God would come get me. I am afraid of a painful death, don't get me wrong. If I am to go, I wanted to go quickly, but I am not afraid of death itself like I was before.

I came back to stay at my home in Waco, Texas, and started congregating in church like I used to. On occasions, my brethren from church would ask me about my experience. I would tell them exactly what I witnessed and what God said. Some would believe it, others not so much, but they would take my word because they knew I was not a liar. I always had a sense of being in "heaven." I had read the book *Heaven Is for Real*. I had heard many testimonials in both English and Spanish from different people going to heaven and describing what it looked like. *It couldn't be heaven*, I thought. But it wasn't hell either. Then, one day, I came across a twenty-minute clip of Pastor John Hagee's sermon about the three heavens. My TV pretty much stayed on the TBN channel. This sparked my interest, and I tried to research more. However, as I kept searching, I discovered that different pastors have different opinions or theories about where the three heavens are. Based on what I found, my experience sounded like I was in the second heaven. So from there on, I would say I visited second heaven.

In my search, I came across 2 Corinthians 12:2–4,

> I know a man in Christ who fourteen years ago was caught up to the third heaven. Whether it was in the body or out of the body I do not know—God knows. And I know that this man—whether in the body or apart from the body I do not know, but God knows—was caught up to paradise and heard inexpressible things, things that no one is permitted to tell.

I thought that this was relatively close to my experience. I felt kind of the same as the man he was describing. Sadly for me, Paul does not continue to say anything else about this man. So once again, I hit a roadblock, so I left it alone. I was taking care of a little baby, so I put all my time and effort into my baby instead of the research. I didn't consider it important enough to press on.

3

CHAPTER

Changing Churches

Around June of 2015, I applied to work for another school district. I was hired to work as a teacher at China Spring High School. My focus then turned to getting ready to start working again. I was very excited to start teaching again. China Spring had a good reputation as being a really good school with good kids. I had one subject to teach all day long, all eight classes, and that was Spanish 2. I really liked this. I had these kids for one year, and then they were off to the next teacher—a big difference from my previous school where I was the only Spanish teacher for the entire school.

The first day of classes, I went over the class rules and expectations, as I had every year since I had become a teacher. The following day, we got to know each other, and I asked them simple questions like "What is your name and age? What is your favorite food? What's your favorite holiday?" And the last question was "Tell me something interesting or unusual about yourself." Everyone in the class answered; some answers were very dry, others loved to talk and elaborated on the answer.

Then, after all the students had answered, it was my turn. I answered all the questions, and when I came across the last one about something interesting or unusual, I said, "I have died and came back to life." The reactions I got were all different; some kids' eyes got bigger, others yelled out, "Wait, what?" I said, "When I was having my baby five months ago, I had an out-of-body experience. I went to a place that I'd like to call second heaven. God spoke to me, and He said that I needed to come back, and I did." It was very, very short and sweet and straight to the point. The entire class was in complete silence and just staring at me. "Questions?" I asked.

Several hands went up, and they asked me all kinds of questions. "What was it like?" "Did you see Jesus?" "What language was God speaking in?" And I would answer them, and more questions would arise from there. I finally stopped when the bell rang. The following class came in and had almost the same reactions. After lunch time, everyone came in expecting to hear the story. In order to not have as many questions, I added a little more when I was telling my story. However, that was the only time I would say anything about my experience because I knew that as a public school teacher, I should not be saying anything about God.

The following year, I did the same thing. The students reacted the same way as the previous year. But this time, I had one student say, "You should write a book." I had never thought about that. I responded to her, "Maybe one day I will." To be honest, I agreed, but I didn't really think I would actually write a book. In my opinion, my experience was just too weird, and I didn't think that it was that important.

I liked teaching, but I wanted to live bolder for God, and working in a public high school, I really couldn't. I had to bite my tongue almost all the time, and when I decided to speak, I would sometimes get called into the office.

The years 2017 and 2018 brought a lot of change in my life—change I was not expecting. February of 2017, my family and I started attending a different church, Antioch Community Church. It was a big change for us; we went from a small Hispanic, Spanish-speaking, and legalistic church to a big English-speaking, liberal, and almost all-white-people church. To be honest, at first, I didn't agree with the church. I liked the church, but according to me, it was a "Christian-lite" church, meaning they didn't preach much about the cross and sin. However, I told God if going to Antioch was His will for me, that I would obey.

I kept on going because I liked the preachings and their kids' ministry is awesome. The church started growing on me, as they say. I started to see things from a different perspective. The people were friendly, and they really loved the Lord. Another thing I liked about the church is that they had a prophetic ministry and occasionally would have trainings or seminars that taught how to walk and grow in prophetic gifting.

The very first training I went to, on April 7, 2017, was about ways of hearing God. I learned that God speaks in different ways. First, through His "Logos," which is his word. Secondly, through an audible voice. This is one very rare, but there are references in Exodus 3:1 when God was speaking to Moses. Thirdly, through dreams and visions. This one was the one I identified with the most. I was able to get many answers that day. I left with many pages of notes from this training. Fourth, through the counsel of friends who really know and love God and those to whom God has given authority in your life. And lastly, fifth, through circumstances—being "caught up" in His will.

Later on, they also had a dream interpretation class. I realized that I am a dreamer, but dream interpretation is not my strong point. It was in these trainings that I met other people like myself and discovered that there were other people just as weird and crazy as me who were also learning to walk in their gifting. Even after all of this, I was still not fully convinced that Antioch was the right path for my family and me.

Sunday mornings, my family and I would have our own church services at home and write our own preachings and sing worship songs. Then we attended Antioch's 5:00 p.m. Spanish service. However, as the weeks progressed, our home services started to die down.

I was confused about what to do; part of me still wanted to go back to my previous church. I missed being involved in all the church activities like the dramas or plays and also playing in a group that we called Eben-Haezer, which was an all-acoustic instruments group that in Spanish we call rondalla. We were not famous by any means; we only played every once in a while in our church. I missed going out to eat with some of the church members after church. You get to know people better when you are in a small church. In a big church, you feel kind of lost if you are not in a small church group or life group.

It was a real struggle for me. I loved my first church. I honestly can't say that I have loved another since that one, but I knew that God was leading me out. I would attend a youth event at my first church; then the following week, I would attend a "Not in My City: Human Trafficking Awareness Event" at Antioch. I really was torn between the two. I spoke with my sister Lilia, and she was listening to the voice of the Holy Spirit that was saying that He was leading me to Antioch. But the doubt was too big.

One Sunday, I was getting ready to go back to my previous church; then at four o'clock in the evening, one hour before the Spanish service at Antioch, I had a thought that came into my mind. *What if I were to give Antioch one last chance?* It was God speaking to me through a thought. I told God: "Father, I am going to give Antioch one last opportunity. If You want me there, You have until today to prove it. If not, this is my last time going."

Yes, I was that daring because I knew that He wouldn't let me down. Sure enough, at the service, I got my response. In the flyers they pass out as you are entering the service, I saw something that popped out at me after the service because I didn't see it until the end. I merely glanced at it and saw "media missions," "creative media and technology for evangelism," "team vision," "praying for people with these giftings to serve with us." These words spoke directly to me. I felt as if God himself was reading the words to me. I went over to the leaders, and I asked them about the flyer. I said, "What does this mean?" They responded that they needed people that knew about video editing and media production because the ones they had were oversaturated with the amount of work they had, and they were praying for more people that could do these things. Well, that was a sign that spoke directly to me. As I was walking out of the church, I felt God give me another thought that said, "You put me to the test, and I responded."

The following day however, doubt came again. "Are you sure it was God?" "What if it was just your emotions?" I was working two jobs at that time. I worked during the day as a high school teacher, and as soon as I got out, I would run to my second full-time job at Cheddar's where I worked as a server. On Wednesday, two days later,

I went to work at Cheddar's, and God sent two men to the restaurant. One of those men entered with a Bible and sat in my section. The one man with a Bible was a white man in his sixties. The first thing he did after I greeted them was ask me, "Is there something you want us to pray for?" I said yes. I wanted to know which direction God wanted me to go. I would obey His command as long as it came from Him. As I heard this man speak, I knew he was filled with the Holy Spirit. It took me twenty minutes just to take their drink order because what he had to say was so important. It was clear to me that God had sent a messenger to give me direction and confirmation that my new church home would now be Antioch.

In between ordering, eating, praying, talking, and me crying, they lasted at that table for two hours. He walked in the gifting of words of knowledge. Something that at that time I did not know about. This man taught me that God will move us where He needs us or where He wants us, even if that place is not where we want to go.

Sometimes God is wanting to take us to a higher knowledge of Himself, but we need to let go of our religiosity to get there. This was definitely a hard lesson for me to learn. I probably would have never dared to walk in words of knowledge or prophecy if I would have stayed in my first church. There's always a reason why God does things. Sometimes we don't know why that reason is until some time has passed.

A few weeks after I left my first church, I saw my previous pastor and his wife at Cheddar's. They did not sit in my section, but I went over to talk to them. "At the end of the day," the pastor said, "The souls don't belong to pastors, they belong to Jesus."

4

CHAPTER

Prophecy Spoken over Me

Being a teacher, I would always talk to my students when they would go through certain situations like heartbreaks, depression, or family problems. I had one student in particular that had recently decided to accept Jesus Christ as her Lord and Savior and started going to church. I can't remember what church she went to, but she wasn't able to go as often as she wanted to because her parents were not believers.

I would have small conversations with her; the majority of the time, it was her asking me questions. Sometimes it would be about Jesus, other times it would be something about the Bible or about the different beliefs among the different denominations. One day, she walks in late to my class and looks like she is about to fall to the ground. I asked her if she was feeling all right, and she responded that she felt very dizzy. In a second, I saw it. I saw something demonic in her arm. I'll try to describe it as much as I can. I saw in her arm a "ball" underneath her skin. It was about the size of a golf ball, only I could see it because I saw it in the spirit. I walked over to her and did the *sh* signal. We were in the back of the room, and all the students' desks were facing the other direction. I took my hand, and I placed it on top of that "ball," and I whispered, "In Jesus's name, be gone." I waited about three seconds with my hand placed there and then removed it. I looked at her and said, "There."

She looked at me with her eyes wide open and said, "Oh my God. Mrs. Parra, oh my God. How did you do that?"

I responded, "Are you feeling better?" She responded that her dizziness was completely gone. I told her to remain quiet about it,

39

at least for the time being. Then, I went up to the front to teach the class. We did talk about it afterward but just in between us.

It was those type of situations, and kids not wanting to learn, that made me question whether I really wanted to continue to be a teacher. I knew I had something that was out of the ordinary, but I was having to put my lamp under a bushel basket. This is a reference to Jesus's words in the Gospel of Matthew. I really wanted to spread my wings and fly, but I couldn't because I was in a public school, and I could be fired.

At that time, I was afraid of being fired. I depended on my salary to pay bills; therefore, I complied, for the most part. The times that I wouldn't, of course, I got called in to the office.

Time passed, and I decided that I did not want to hide my light, and I wanted to pursue ministry. So I thought. I didn't know what that was going to look like. I just knew I had to walk in that direction and trust God that he would lead me somewhere different. I told my principal that I would not be coming back the following year. I told him that I wanted a job outside of teaching.

I told God to open doors where He wanted me to go and to close the paths that were not for me. I applied at different places. I thought I had many options to choose from. I would get responses from those jobs, but those roads did not lead to employment. Every door I tried ended up being a closed door. I was now getting a little worried. The problem was that I wanted a job that paid the same amount as a teacher, not less.

Aren't we all like that? We think that it's only a blessing if we are going up on the economic ladder. I would pray to God, and I would ask Him for a different job with the same amount of money or preferably more money. I could've had a different job if I would have conformed to a smaller paycheck. However, I didn't want that. I need a different college degree, I thought.

I wanted full time ministry, but I still needed to pay my bills. So what did I do? As embarrassed as I am to admit it, I went back to teaching. It was almost time for the next school year to start, one week prior to be exact. I was holding on to one job that I felt I really wanted until August, but it ended up being a dead end. So I applied at Waco ISD and got hired right away. I felt relieved that I would have an income. Waco ISD is one of the highest-paying school districts in the area. I was relieved, for the time being, because I had a financial cushion now, but it was not the ministry I was longing for.

Then one night, I had a dream. I dreamed that I was in a school teaching and that I was joyful and the kids would hug me as they left to go home. However, these children that I saw in my dream were shorter, or younger, than the normal high school students I was accustomed to. I liked that dream. I thought, *Well, if God can give me the joy of teaching again, then I guess I can do this.*

Once I got hired at the school, I thought I could keep working at the restaurant, just like I had for years. But this job was more demanding and more stressful. I was too tired at the end of the day to go to another fast-paced job. I didn't understand where the tiredness came from. After all, I had worked two jobs for years, and I was used to it. I decided to let go of my restaurant job and only stick with teaching.

During the beginning of that fall semester in 2017, I was in the college service at church, and I was serving with the tech team as the video producer. We were all feeling the presence of the Holy Spirit when suddenly, I had a vision. I had my eyes opened, and I saw a motion picture as I like to call it—Carlos, Adonaldo, and I were in Africa, and Carlos was teaching the children how to play soccer. It was more of a friendly match than actual teaching. I was sitting on the ground with Adonaldo near me watching Carlos and the children play. I could see the color of the dirt, the grass, and the type of vegetation. The vision lasted about three seconds, and it ended.

Since that moment, I started to believe that God would send us to Africa one day. I believed it wholeheartedly. I got home after church and told Carlos about it. He didn't really believe me; he knew that I had said crazy things before, and they all turned out to be true. So he would always think twice before dismissing anything I said. I was very excited to see what God was going to do, and I was eager to get going.

On October 6 and 7 of 2017, Antioch had its first Enciende conference. It was a two-day conference broken up into four sessions.

It was in Spanish, but they did offer English translation. I was very excited for this conference. I was serving with the tech team on the light board this time. I love all the techy stuff, by the way. This date is so important to me. We had three speakers for the conference: Carlos Rodriguez, David Karnes, and Duene Kershner.

The first session was a lovely preaching about God's grace and love. Then David Karnes's turn came up, and he also gave a very good message. His message spoke to me in the area of marriage. The very last session was for Duene Kershner. I had no idea who he was or anything behind his ministry prior to this conference.

When the worship stopped during his session, he did not stand in the front like all the other preachers. He walked back and forth in the front area just looking at the people that were there. He started explaining about his work at Roca Blanca Mission Base in Mexico. He would stop and all of the sudden would point to a certain person and say, "You. God wants to speak to you," and right then and there he would say a word of knowledge to that person. I am a witness that he did not speak to any of those people before this session. He said the word of knowledge or the prophecy and would continue to preach. He would talk about God's goodness in between his prophecies or words of knowledge. I rarely saw preachings like this on TV or on my phone, but I had never seen it in person. The pianist in the worship team kept playing for another thirty minutes. Duene kept on searching for more people. He would say things like "I am looking to see who God signals to me." I was marveled at how he had divine revelation of people he had never seen before. I wish every preaching would be like that, an on-the-spot demonstration of the power and wisdom of God.

He signaled out my father. I was shocked and very excited. I quickly grabbed my phone and video recorded as much as I could. He said to him that God was going to send him to preach to his family members the message of salvation. He placed his hands on my father's head, and my father started to shake. That doesn't happen too often.

How does God tell him? How does Duene hear God? When he says he "sees," how does he see it? How is he able to see angels in the room? I was both amazed and curious. I wanted to do it too. He continued to preach and give divine revelations. At the end of it all, he did an altar call, and many responded. I was in the back and couldn't go up because I was working the lights, but I really wanted to go to the front. I saw my parents come toward me, thinking they were going to tell me something, but they had gone back to get me and take me to the front. We walked in between all the people there and went directly to Duene. My father said to Duene, "This is my daughter." Duene looked at me for about five seconds, took a deep breath, and placed his hands on my head. He said to my father (speaking about me), "Your daughter will be used greatly, your daughter will see visions, your daughter will lay hands on the sick, and they will recover. Your daughter will prophesy." I was so filled with joy.

I would say in my head, *Yes, I want that, Father.* I fell to the ground after that with a big smile on my face. I desired every single word that came out of his mouth. I wanted to be used greatly by God. After I fell to the ground, Duene went onto the next person. After about a minute or two, I got up and went back to my light board station. I believed it wholeheartedly. Every single word that he said, I took it to heart and desired it. I couldn't wait for that time to come.

The following year, Antioch hosted another Enciende, but they didn't bring back Duene. All the preachings were great, but none of the preachers prophesied or said any words of knowledge in their preachings. They did afterward when the people came up to respond to the altar call. So in my opinion, it wasn't as good.

Two days later on October 9 and 10, 2017, I was sent by the school to Houston, Texas, for a two-day AVID workshop. I stayed at a hotel paid for by the school. I really enjoyed being alone during those two days. It gave me time to think and watch TV and do things I hadn't been able to do since I had my son.

On the drive back, I was thinking that I would have to sell the house and all my belongings to be able to travel to wherever God was going to send us. Before this, I would never have thought of selling the house nor relocating to any other place.

I was all in, with my faith very high. However, there was still one impediment—Carlos. I knew that if the vision were to come to pass, Carlos would need to fix his immigration papers. I took it as a sign that we had to get to work on adjusting his immigration status. We had consulted one immigration attorney a few years back, and he told us that through USCIS, he would not be able to adjust his status. We were shocked and a little heartbroken that he didn't give us any hope. We left it alone for years and waited to see if immigration law changed over time.

"If God said it, He will do it," I told Carlos. With this new-found hope, we decided to consult other lawyers. We drove to San Antonio to consult with a different attorney. We were once again told that he wouldn't be able to qualify for any of the routes established by USCIS. This attorney at least told us that there was one way, and that was to get detained by immigration officials, or ICE, and fight his case in court. We said to the attorney that we thought it was a bad idea because what if they didn't grant him permission, then he would get deported to Mexico. We drove back home feeling a little down, but I was not giving up because I knew God was going to work on our behalf. We would joke about it afterward and say that he should let himself be caught to see what happens.

I knew God would do something miraculous and Carlos would be legal in the United States. My only solution was to turn to the only person that I knew could do something about it—God. I said to God that if we were to do as His vision showed me, that He was going to have to help us get Carlos his green card.

I decided to investigate for myself what it was going to take to get him legal status. In college, I had done two research papers on immigration policies, and I had previously helped friends file the paperwork necessary to USCIS for their green card. Their cases were the easy ones, of course, and they were all approved. However, immigration law is constantly changing, and Carlos's case was not an easy one. It wasn't easy because he had three entrances to the country, and USCIS can only waive, or forgive, one entrance.

"I'm going to need you to take the wheel on this," I would say to God. Going to see immigration attorneys is not cheap, so I tried to look at all the free routes first. On October 16, we went once again to San Antonio to the US Citizenship and Immigration Services office to ask the immigration clerks or attendants for information on what path Carlos could take. This was a free route. I was able to enter because I am an American citizen; Carlos had to stay in the truck. We left Waco at three in the morning to make sure we arrived by six to get in line. I was there by six fifteen and waited in line until they opened the doors at seven. The morning was cold, and the line was very long. I was the fourth one in line. The first one in line had been there since 5:00 a.m.

I finally went in, and I explained to the immigration clerks our situation. "There has to be something that can be done," I would say. I explained to them that his father had petitioned him when he was a child, and everything was approved all the way up to the very last appointment in Juarez. His father didn't have the money to pay, and he abandoned the case on the day he would have received his green card. The person I spoke to did not have much of a clue about what I should do. He gave me vague answers that didn't match what I was asking him. At the end of the conversation, he advised me that for difficult cases, like Carlos's, that I should consult an attorney. All those hours of driving for twenty minutes of being in front of this person, and I still left empty handed.

However, I didn't give up, and I would research as much as I could in my free time, which was almost nonexistent due to work and having my little one, Adonaldo, at home. I had purposed myself to know what an attorney would know in reference to Carlos's case. I learned some legal terminology while trying to find a path for Carlos. Almost all routes led to a dead end. I wanted God to operate in my timing; more particularly, I wanted Him to do it fast. However, God doesn't operate on our time. He knows exactly when He needs to act.

I kept having faith, but I almost gave up. Waiting on a promise from God is not easy. I wish I could say that faith is easy, but it is not. It is very hard. It is hard to hang on to what God has said when your surroundings say the opposite. But if we endure standing on God's word, then we will prevail.

5
CHAPTER

The Ups and Downs

On October 21, 2017, I went to another prophetic training at Antioch. I wrote down as much as I could, and as fast as I could, to try to retain as much as possible. I had set my mind that if God had said that He was going to use me in a certain area or gifting, then I needed to prepare myself and learn about those giftings. This was on top of the immigration research I was doing.

It was a lot to take in. I ended my work day at 5:00 p.m. feeling very tired and ready to go to bed. I thought I was getting so stressed with everything that it was making me sick. *Something is not normal,* I thought. Then, I tried to remember when my last period was, and it had been over a month. *Wait a second,* I thought, *could it be?* On October 29, I took a pregnancy test and found out I was pregnant. I couldn't believe it. It was such a surprise.

I had told God previously that I would leave it in His hands if He wanted to give me another child or not and that I was no longer going to worry or ask for another child. It would be His will if it happened. And it did.

Carlos and I were very happy that God had granted us another child, but I was not looking forward to the pregnancy symptoms. *If this pregnancy is like the other one, I am going to have to quit my job,* I thought. However, this pregnancy was not as bad as the last one. When I went back to my OB-GYN, they did an ultrasound to see how far along I was because I had no idea. I was six weeks pregnant. I did some calculations, and I got pregnant some time before the conference in Houston. It happened during the time I was believing for change. It wasn't the change I was expecting, but it was a surprise.

In reference to the pregnancy symptoms, I still had nausea, but I didn't have as much vomiting as I did during my first pregnancy. Of course, there were those days that I didn't feel well, and I would stay home, but I still continued to go to work. One day I remember being at school and feeling very nauseous. I wanted to vomit, so I ran to the bathroom but I didn't quite make it to the sink. I made a mess. God bless the custodians at school; they are much appreciated.

After I got pregnant, I did absolutely the bare minimum as a teacher. I couldn't do more. I was proud of myself for continuing to go to work. Something I couldn't do in my first pregnancy. To be honest, I felt like the dreams and hopes I had were turning out to be not true. I was not seeing a path for Carlos's green card, I was not going to Africa, and I was not getting the joy of teaching as I had dreamed.

Did I fail? Was it just a regular dream and I confused it with a prophetic dream? My faith was tested. Was I still going to believe even though I didn't get an immediate answer? Over the years, I have learned to be a little more patient, but for the most part, I am impatient. I want quick responses, I want my prayers to be answered right away, so God has had to teach me to be patient time and time again.

In times of uncertainty, I must keep going and keep walking. I did not dismiss what God told me or what He showed me in visions. The answer was to keep walking and keep trusting. When students would ask me what I wanted the gender of the baby to be, I would respond that I wanted another boy. Carlos also wanted another boy, but we both said that whatever God decided to give us, we would be grateful.

I had to change my OB-GYN, not because I didn't want my previous doctor to continue my care, but because she didn't accept Medicare. Although I was doubting whether to continue with her or not. I was fortunate enough to qualify for Texas's Medicare for pregnant women, which typically covers pregnancy, childbirth, and some postnatal care.

It was during this chaos that I had another important dream. I dreamed that I was in the hospital giving birth to my baby. I saw the baby after the nurses gave it a bath, and I was able to stand up. It was a boy. I was excited that I had another baby boy. However, as I looked at him, I started to notice that something was not right about the baby. I got suspicious if it was my baby because it looked like a four-month-old baby; it was too big to be a newborn. My happiness soon turned into confusion. I told the nurses that this baby couldn't possibly be mine. They said, "Well maybe there was a mix-up or something," and in a hurry, they went to try to find answers. Next to him was another baby, and it also didn't look like it could be mine because he looked Asian. I turned back to the baby they said was mine, and he looked like a white baby, and I was even more convinced that it wasn't my baby. I walked some more, and I came across a tiny baby girl lying in a hospital bassinet pushed all the way to the wall. I looked at her; she was very small, very peaceful, and quiet. She did have a darker tone to her skin than the baby boy. I picked her up and placed her in my arms. It felt like a perfect fit. She was my lost baby; I had found her. The room then turned into a very dimly lighted nursery, where only me and her were in the room. She was a lot smaller than Adonaldo as a newborn. My dream ended, and I can still remember this so clearly. I told Carlos that if the dream was correct, we were going to have a baby girl. However, we both still wanted a boy. I had to wait once again to know if the dream was prophetic or not. God likes to use us in our weak spots to show His strength.

Since I was pregnant, I decided to pause the immigration research. I figured I was not going on any missionary trip to Africa for the time being, so I concentrated on my pregnancy, and I took it day by day.

I practiced as much as I could to hear God for myself and for other people in church. As we prayed about any topic, I would bypass that and ask God to supernaturally tell me something about someone that was close to me. Fifty percent of the time, He would. If He did, then I would freak out because now I had the responsibility to share it with them. Another thing about me is that even though it might not look like it, I am actually very shy, and I always overthink things. I was afraid of the word being only a thought in my head and not God. "There is only one way to find out," I would say to myself. On occasions, the thought was so far out there that I didn't have the courage to share. If it was a simple and good word, I would share. I once gave a word of knowledge to a young college boy that I saw him going to Brazil and praying very powerfully for people. I didn't know what he was actually looking into that. Ever since that day, I fell in love with words of knowledge. It is one of the hardest gifts to walk in, in my opinion. But I kept it up, and I would try to practice every time I could. When I would go by myself to the store, and I would be walking behind someone. I would ask God for a word for that person. He would not always answer. As a matter of fact, I would rarely get an answer from Him. If I did, I would still ask for confirmation before I shared it. I wasn't ready. I was bold but not bold enough at that time.

December came around, and Antioch was hosting a Christine D'Clario concert in Spanish. I was once again serving during the event in greeting people that came in and helping sell her merchandise before and after her concert. But I was able to sneak in for a good while and to see her concert. During that concert, I felt another God impression. I had a thought that came into my head that said that this baby in my womb was going to be a sort of Christine D'Clario. I said, "Lord, whatever you want this baby to be, let it be so, as long as this baby is doing it for your kingdom." I still remember this sweet impression. I will have to wait many years to see whether this one comes true or not.

Christmastime came around; it was the Christmas year that my two sisters and I were pregnant. Yes, my sister Lilia, my sister Natalia (recently married), and I were pregnant. Talk about a blessing.

It was during this time that I started to grow in visions. I was growing in the "seeing" not just the "hearing." I would close my eyes, and in the dark canvas before me, I would see tones of light. On occasions, I would see different tones of brown or a warm yellow-colored light. Months later, I would see "motion pictures" in full color. However, here I would only see tones of brown or yellow light that formed an image. It was not a still image. It was like watching a slow-motion video. I normally would say to the people there what I just saw, but on occasions, it was difficult to explain because it wasn't the norm to see that in the natural world, so I would draw it. I would see a lot of nature in my visions. I would see mountains, rivers, trees, or sometimes images like a little girl swinging in an outside swing. I kept praying for God to keep on using me in that matter. I only asked for these visions when I was in a Bible study group or at church. It was only among the people that were believers, or my family, that I would speak about my visions. I wanted to get a vision for a complete stranger out in the grocery store, but I considered it too risky. I didn't really hang out with any nonbelievers, so my entire circle were people of faith, and it was with them that I would practice receiving visions or words for.

February 1, 2018, Carlos and I went to my ultrasound appointment. We didn't care about gender reveals; we wanted to know right then the gender of the baby. Carlos and I were still hoping for a baby boy, but I kind of had a feeling that it was going to be a girl. Then the baby sonographer, or the ultrasound technician, said the words "It's a girl."

"Are you sure?" I asked.

"Yes, I can see the girl parts very clearly." To be honest, I was a little sad, but I was still happy. There's an old superstitious belief among the Mexican culture that a mother has to be very careful on wanting, or desiring, a gender of the baby because if the mother is really wanting a girl and it turns out to be a boy, then that boy might have some feminine behaviors or turn out to be gay. The same applies for the girls, just the opposite. I know it sounds crazy, but that really is the belief. Therefore, the purpose of this belief is that as a mother, you were to remain neutral about desiring a gender and just be thankful for whatever God gave you. With that in mind, once I found out that it was a girl, I discarded the desire of a baby boy. I went to Walmart and bought a big "It's a Girl" banner to hang in my class for the students to see. It was so much fun seeing the students come in and celebrating.

Within that week, my health started to change. My blood pressure started to go up to dangerous numbers. I went to the nurse and said, "I feel like my heart is trying to come out of my chest. Could you check my pulse or my blood pressure, please?" The school nurse checked it and said that it was 180 over 120. I thought I was feeling fine except for the heart racing. I did have a history of hypertension, so it didn't surprise me. She said that I needed to go to the hospital. I thought that she was exaggerating and that it couldn't be that bad. I said I just need to lay down for a little bit and let my heart rate calm down; then, I'll be fine. However, minutes transpired, and I didn't get much better. The nurse said that she had to send me home at the very least, that she couldn't in good conscience let me stay at work. She really wanted to send me to the hospital, but I said no. The same scenario happened again the following days, and each time, I was sent home. I went to the doctor, and I was prescribed some medication. I was able to keep the numbers a little lower and at least remain at school.

However, the damage was done, the female principal had enough of me, and she called me into the office and said that she was going to have to write me up and that it was going to go on my record. I said, "No, it's not. I'd rather quit than have that on my record." I left for the day and turned in my resignation letter the following day, which was just three sentences long. It was the middle of February, and there were twelve weeks left of the school year. I really wanted to finish out the year because I did not want to break my contract, but the principal wasn't having it.

I was a bit relieved because now I didn't have to go to work, and I could concentrate on getting my health back on track, for my sake and my baby's sake. On the contrary, however, now we had to rely only on Carlos's job. He had his own landscaping and remodeling business that he was starting. On some days, he would have work, and the check would be good, but on other days, there would be nothing. It wasn't a steady income.

"Now what happened?" I would ask God. It seemed like another failure, once again. I went from thinking that I would go flying around the world to being pregnant and without a job. Not to mention the dangerous blood pressure levels. I couldn't understand it. However, I remained in belief, I remained in prayer, I remained reading my Bible and watching Christian television. I'm so thankful for those times in the Bible where the character, or the person, is going through a tragedy or something difficult because I'm able to relate to that when I'm going through tragedies or difficult times. I'm so thankful for the preachers that preach on these topics.

Shortly after I resigned, a full-time position opened up at Antioch with the Spanish ministry. I immediately applied. I thought that this was it, this was the reason I had to leave teaching; I was trying to make sense of it all with my human reasoning. Well weeks passed, and I didn't get the job. I was heartbroken, not necessarily because I didn't get the job but because I was back to the confusion of not knowing what was to come next. I was at an all-time high spiritually speaking, but in the natural, I was down. I had to press through and see the good in all of it. The good in it was that I was now able to stay at home with Adonaldo, I was able to attend church activities that were during the day, and just relax from the stress of my previous job.

We had to think of a name for the baby girl. I was thinking of Emily because in the dream, the baby's name was Emily, but Carlos didn't want that name. So we went back to the big book of baby names, and I searched there. I wanted a name that was short, no more than five letters, and that sounded feminine. More particularly a name that my three-year-old son, Adonaldo, could pronounce. While I was still looking at names that began with an A, I read "Alia." I liked it. It sounded pretty; it was feminine, short, and my son could pronounce it. *Alia* is a Hebrew name that means rising, ascending, royalty, or princess. When I chose it, I did not know it was a name derived from the Hebrew origin until now that I am writing this book, which is totally awesome.

The months passed, and two weeks before my scheduled C-section, my sister had her baby boy. I was next. We had the date set for June 1, 2018, three weeks before my actual due date so that there would be no chances of me going into labor. If I attempted to have the baby naturally, I could probably die trying.

The night before my scheduled C-section, I prayed to God to have the delivery as normal as possible. I wasn't complaining about my previous experience, but I did not want to go through that again. The time came, and I was checked into the hospital. This time around, it was entirely different. I remember complaining that my scheduled time was at 8:00 a.m., and it was already past 9:00, and I still hadn't been passed to the operating room.

Once the process began, everything went well. Carlos was able to be by my side, and I was awake and alert the entire time. Once they put the epidural or the spinal anesthesia on and I started to feel the numbing coming up to my chest area, I would get a little nervous, and the memories would come back. However, I tried to control my emotions and my thoughts so that I wouldn't freak out. My doctor was telling me step by step what was happening and what was to come next. Deep breaths, I was glad I was able to take deep breaths this time. In just a few minutes, Alia was out, and I was able to see her shortly. Since I was approved for Medicare, I decided to take advantage of it and get my tubes cut and burned. I did not want to go through another pregnancy again, plus I only wanted two kids. My doctor explained to me that there was a possibility that I could still become pregnant. I said, "Well, if that's the case, then it would be God's will.

We were moved to a regular room shortly after. When I saw Alia, she was tiny just like in my dream. She was born at 10:33 a.m. and weighed 6 pounds and 0.3 ounces. She was, after all, three weeks early, but even though she was early, she was still small. We were kept a little longer in the hospital to check on my progress due to what happened to me last time. They were very cautious with me. Three days later we were released from the hospital. We were glad to be going home.

6

CHAPTER

Get Ready, You Are about to Move

The weeks and months passed. I decided to keep on staying home after I had Alia. If I would have returned to work, I would've had to pay at least $800 a month for day care. So I kept staying at home with my little ones. The money was so tight that I decided to apply for food stamps and was approved. That was a blessing. I also worked at home doing a little video editing. Mr. Quiroga would get hired to video record eight-hour long, or longer, events like weddings, baptisms, and quinceañeras, and then he would bring the recordings in a cassette to me. I would have to turn it into digital format first, then edit the video, putting any graphics or special effects in places. I also had to do picture editing to design a DVD cover for the cases they would go in. I had a kind of printer that would allow me to print on top of the DVDs, so I had to design that as well. I had been doing this for him for more than three years, but it was only when he was hired for a job. Eventually, he was persuaded to get a digital camera. That helped me do the work a little faster. This was a lot of work for a little money. I only charged him $80 per event. Eventually, I bumped it up to $100, still very cheap. I didn't complain because I liked video editing and all the techy stuff. Since I was a stay-at-home mom, I had the time to wait for the video rendering times and the DVD burning times.

It was interesting to me that when we were very low on money, Mr. Quiroga would come in with up to three jobs to do at a time. God was teaching me to keep going and to trust in Him. He was showing me that He would accommodate all things. He was teach-

54

ing me to be faithful in the little and in the very little. Keep the faith when you are poor and barely making it, keep the faith when you have everything or are well off, keep the faith when you can't see what tomorrow will bring, just keep the faith that He will guide us through it all.

Alia was born with an umbilical hernia that caused her belly button to bulge out. Her doctor would examine it and said that it should go away on its own. With the passing of the months, the bulging did start to go down, so it seemed like she was not going to need surgery. That was another blessing from God.

Saturday September 1, 2018, I was driving down a big road in town that was on the top of a hill. As I was waiting at a traffic light, I looked at the sky. It was such a pretty sky. There were some small clouds that seemed to somewhat hide the sun, but there were areas where the sun would pass through the clouds. That light coming in through the clouds made the sky look beautiful. I normally don't look up while I'm driving, but I felt the need to look up.

While I was looking at the sky, I heard the voice of God in my thoughts that said, "Get ready because you are about to move." That was it, just a thought that came into my mind with a male tone to it. I didn't know what to think of it. I knew that it was not my head or my emotions because I was not thinking about anything related. I grabbed my phone and took a picture of the sky. I still have that picture today. The light turned green, and I continued to drive away. That was one of the few times that I was not in prayer when God spoke to me, and that was probably the clearest I have ever heard him.

I went home and told Carlos; he didn't really believe me. Due to our current financial situation, a move was not in our plans. We were falling behind on our home and vehicle payments. I am so thankful for my parents during that time; at times we wouldn't have enough for the electric bill or the water bill, and they would let us borrow money.

We kept falling deeper and deeper into a financial hole that I couldn't see how we were going to get out of it. I cried out to God for help. I said, "God, help Carlos's business grow so he can make more money." However, as the weeks passed, it seemed that God was not answering my prayers; he had less and less jobs. Part of it was because it was getting close to the wintertime, and landscaping jobs are not as abundant. Another part of it was because He had a different plan in mind. I once again felt like a failure. It was this roller coaster of circumstances that never seemed to stabilize over the years.

I continued to be involved in church activities. I would volunteer with the homeless outreach. When you think you have hit bottom, go help out with the homeless and listen to their problems, and you will soon see that what you are going through is nothing in comparison. I met a couple while serving with this outreach. They slept on the park floor under a tree. The woman was eight months pregnant. I wanted to help them get out of that situation. I drove them to different organizations in town. I learned a lot during this time about how difficult it is to get out of being homeless. I would always come back to God and say, "I am complaining too much. I still have a house to live in and food to eat. Therefore, I have something to be thankful for."

My sister Natalia had moved to Fort Stockton, Texas, with her husband after she got married. My brother-in-law worked for an oil field company. On one of their visits to Waco, he showed me one of his paycheck stubs. It was a decent amount of money. I said to him that he made more money because he was sort of a manager. He did some calculations, and he said to me that Carlos could be making around $2,000 or more biweekly. "That would be great right now," I said, "but he doesn't have his papers." He said that he was also working on getting his papers but that he was thankful to his father who had petitioned for his social security when he was a child. That sparked something in me. A spark of hope.

I didn't know if Carlos would agree to this kind of job or not, but I felt a window of opportunity being opened. I called Carlos and asked him if he would be interested in working at the oil field and he said yes. Later that day, I asked if he was in the same situation as my brother-in-law in reference to his social security. He said that he believed his father had also gotten him a social security number as a child, but he wasn't sure.

Desperate to find answers, we went to his father's house, and I asked all kinds of immigration questions. I was able to get copies of all the paperwork that immigration had sent to his father. The big packet that he gave us included approved petitions from immigration and important numbers like his alien number. We also found his social security card. We were so excited for this new information that we had recently discovered. We realized the hard truth that he would have been a resident by now if his father would have followed through. Not only would Carlos have been a resident but three of his siblings as well. It was a hard pill to swallow, but we couldn't change the past. His father cried and apologized to Carlos; it was a very emotional moment.

With this newfound information, Carlos was now able to apply for the job at the same company that my brother-in-law worked at. This was around mid-October when all of this happened. I began to mobilize everything. I activated my faith like never before. I was not even certain that Carlos would get hired at the company, but I took hold of this as if it was going to happen no matter what. I started to sell everything we had online. I sold our beds, our kitchen table and appliances, our living room furniture, and we donated a lot of clothes. I got rid of everything except for the few clothes we needed. The reason I needed to get rid of everything was because, if this worked out, we were going to live with my sister in her new RV.

Carlos, Alia, Adonaldo, and I were going to live in a small room that was about twelve feet by ten feet, meaning all our belongings had to fit in this one area. Finally, three days later, we got a response, and he was hired. We were so happy. I was jumping with joy. I said to Carlos, "See, I told you so." They said they wanted him there next week. We had one week to let go of the rest of the stuff and move. Fort Stockton is about seven hours away from Waco. It was going to be a long drive to a place we had never seen or visited before.

The house we were buying was an owner finance. I am so thankful that God placed the owner of that house in our path. He was a good God-fearing man, and he was more than patient with us. I've heard horror stories of people that get into owner finance contracts, and years later, they discover that it was all a scam. Thank God that was not our case. We made an agreement, and we sold the house back to him. We didn't get any money out of the sale, which we were okay with. Now it was Carlos's turn to sell all his tools and landscaping equipment. It was a hard thing for him to do. I could see it in his face. He was a little slower than me at selling everything. He really wanted to have his own business, but he knew that the best thing for the family was to move. I had bought several things for Alia like a crib and other things that she never got to use because we had to turn around and give them away.

In those last days, our light and our water was cut off due to nonpayment. I don't know how we could have kept going in that situation. The last day we were in the house, it was raining. The day was painted in gray, there was no sunshine. I was so glad that God had provided a way out.

We finally got everything sold, and we were out of the house on Saturday, October 20. The next day, Sunday, at ten in the morning, we loaded our kids, the little clothing we had, our dog, and the little baby stuff we had in the truck and headed out to Fort Stockton, Texas. I was able to see the change in the terrain as we drove further west.

Carlos was supposed to start that Monday, but he ended up starting the following week, which gave us time to go and see the town a little bit. I was very thankful to God for this opportunity.

The place where we parked the RV was at the end of the town. There were no more houses to one side. I could sit by one of the windows and just contemplate the view. It is an area with flat terrain, but in a distance, I could see several mesas. There were not many trees around; it was mostly the short juniper and some lotebush, if that's what it's called. There was hardly any grass, so when the wind blew, it would cause a lot of dirt to rise up. That was something we had to get used to, that and the no trees.

Every morning, my sister and I would get up early and make the men their breakfast and lunch. They would leave sometime before seven. My sister after cooking would go back to sleep, but I couldn't go back to sleep. I would make myself a coffee and eat a little of what was left over as my breakfast. My kids were still asleep, so I would take advantage of the quietness and use that time to talk to God.

Even though we were two families living in one RV, it wasn't that bad because it was mostly my sister and I with three little ones. The thing about Fort Stockton is that there are not many apartments or houses for rent. A lot of people live in RVs. There were more RV parks than apartment complexes. So as much as I tried to find a home or an apartment for rent, there were none. I knew that God was with us. I could feel Him in my morning talks. I wouldn't necessarily pray eloquent prayers; I just sat at the table and talked to Him in my thoughts, as if I was speaking to another person. He was my best friend and the only "person" that was always there.

It was during this season of my life that my visions and dreams grew. I was regularly having these visions and dreams that I had to start writing them down. However, I was really bad at remembering to write them down. It all depended on what time the kids would get up or if it was small enough to write it before I had to get up to make Carlos's lunch. Most of the time, I wouldn't write them.

On October 29, something I'd like to call a miracle happened. I had served myself some hot water in a cup, and I left it on the table to go get the instant coffee to pour in the water. Alia was about to be five months old, and she was at that stage where she grabbed everything that was in front of her. So as soon as I turned around, she grabbed the top of the cup, and she spilled part of the water. Carlos was able to stop her from spilling all of it. My first thought was, *Oh my god, she is going to get burned. Dios mio, Dios mio.* I was wearing flip-flops, and I felt a little bit of water splash on my feet. The water felt cool and not hot.

I was almost certain that her little hand was burned because all the water that spilled passed through her hand. I grabbed her hand, and it was dry. Then I checked her torso and legs, and they were dry. I took her out of her seat and checked all her clothing to see if she was wet in any area, and she was still completely dry. I could not explain it. I checked the cup again, and it had less water, but the vapor was still coming out of it. I thought, *"Maybe the water somehow fell to the side or maybe the water is not hot anymore."* I put my finger in it and felt the heat, and I checked all the area for water but there was none. That's when I realized that something supernatural had happened. It was divine protection. I saw the water falling, and I felt a few drops fall on my feet. It still amazes me today. The water somehow vanished in thin air. We all felt angels around us during that season of our lives. Sometimes it is in the lowest moments where you can sense God with you the most.

Every morning, I loved to look outside and watch the sun come up. I took a picture on my phone to try to get the beauty of the sunrise coming up in the horizon. When I looked at the picture, I saw that the focus was not on the sunrise but on the waterdrops on the window. I felt God saying to me, "Focus on what's in front of you, not on what's to come." God was still teaching me patience.

We went back to Waco for the Thanksgiving holiday and for Alia's six-month medical checkup. During that visit, thanks to my parents, we bought an RV for us to live in so we could move out of my sister's RV. It was a used 2017 model, but we were very happy to be getting it. It had what I wanted and how I wanted it. It is a thirty-foot travel trailer, also known as a bumper pull; it is not a fifth wheel. It had everything we needed to live in. I have always called it an RV even though I know it is a travel trailer. Around mid-December, we went back to Fort Stockton with our new home—our RV, one that we still live in today.

When the new year came around, I decided to start digging more into the word and pressing more into the Holy Spirit. After I sent Carlos off to work with his lunch, I would sit in the quietness and read the Bible. I had a system going. I would read five chapters of the Bible; then, I would read one chapter of any of the other books. At one time, I was reading three books aside from the Bible. Those were some fun times. I had as much time as the kids would allow me before they woke up.

In the beginning of March, we decided to go visit Waco for spring break. I was determined to get started on Carlos's immigration paperwork. I said to God, "God, I trust You. I am going to do this, and I want Your help as I figure this out. Reveal to me, Father, what is the path for his green card." I decided to take advantage of my parents' Internet and their babysitting to sit in front of the computer and research exactly what needed to be filed. Now having the information from the paperwork my father-in-law had given to us, I called several times the USCIS hotline to try to get answers, but each person I spoke to would give me a different answer.

It was time to go back to Fort Stockton, so I told Carlos that I needed more time to use the computer and do research. We agreed that I and the kids would stay behind, and he would return to Fort Stockton with my sister and my brother-in-law. They were both traveling in their different trucks. My plan of action was to fill out the normal I-130, Petition for Alien Relative. I was going to send it and pray to God that it would get approved. I was going to pray over the papers before I sent them and really get on my knees and pray for that to succeed. I knew that was a long shot, but that was the only thing I could do. Or so I thought.

Well, almost four hours after they left Waco, close to Eldorado, Texas, a police officer stopped Carlos for speeding. Carlos was passing up some bikers, and as he was speeding to pass them up, the police officer saw him and stopped him. It's always risky when an illegal immigrant gets stopped by the police because the police officer could give you a ticket and send you on your way or he could take you to ICE. Well, this particular officer decided to take him in and wait for ICE. My sister was the one that called me and said that he was being taken into custody by Eldorado police. There's two things that could have happened, one is that they could release him after a few hours or he is left there until the ICE agents go pick him up to deport him. I was very worried, and I prayed that he would get released. Several hours later, Carlos called me. He said that the plan was to take him and not release him.

The following day, I had this thought suddenly come to my mind. He needs to get detained by ICE, and he needs to go to an immigration detention center. It was the Holy Spirit telling me that what was happening was actually the only pathway to become a resident. Then, I remembered what one lawyer had said to us, that the only way to get his status adjusted was to take his case to the immigration courts. We would have to go before a judge and win the case, of course, in order for his immigration status to be adjusted. I had discarded that idea as too risky, but God knew what I didn't. If

I would have sent those forms to USCIS, they probably would have been rejected, and we would have lost all our money. Even though the situation looked bad, God was actually protecting us and purifying us. In Bible times, refiners used fire as a gold purifier. Fire caused impurities to rise to the surface. When all the impurities are gone, you have 24-karat gold, which is the most valuable grade.

When Carlos called me the next day, he sounded very worried and down. I told him to let the immigration officers take him. I told him that it was actually a good thing this happened and advised him to not sign his voluntary departure. I told him that it was necessary for his case to be taken before the judge. He was only allowed to talk for a few minutes.

He was in that jail for a total of three days. He was then transported to another holding facility closer to the border, where he remained for about a week. I could call the immigration officers to see if he was still detained there, but I had no communication with him. I knew that he would later be taken to the final destination, an immigration detention center in Pearsall, Texas. There the judges decide who gets deported and who gets out on bond. Due to the caravans of migrants coming in through the border, what should have taken three days tops took two weeks. It was a tough two weeks.

I received a call that we could go pick up his truck from Eldorado. My father drove me and my two children four hours to the garage where they were holding it. We paid the fees and were able to drive it away. My father returned to Waco, and I took the truck and my kids and drove to Fort Stockton. That night, I got a call from Carlos saying that he was in the detention center in Pearsall, Texas. It was such a huge relief, not only because they had finally taken him but also because I was worried that he would get too anxious and sign his voluntary departure. We could not do anything to help his case until he was there.

Now that he was in Pearsall, I could look for an attorney and try to see what the next step was. So I got in contact with the same attorney agency from San Antonio that told us that he would need to go through the immigration court and plead his case. The following morning, I drove from Fort Stockton to San Antonio with Alia and Adonaldo. It should normally be a five hour drive, but I had to stop regularly because I was still breastfeeding Alia, and there was no telling when Adonaldo needed to go to the restroom. It was just the three of us making this journey. We finally arrived in San Antonio, and I signed all the contracts, paid two thousand dollars, and the attorney was going to get to work on his case.

I decided to go back to Waco instead of going to Fort Stockton. Yet another four-hour drive with a baby and a three-year-old in the back of the truck. It was nighttime when we got home. That was a lot on the kids. But at least now, I could stay put, and I was closer to San Antonio if I ever needed to go. I also needed my parents' Internet.

At least now we could go visit him, and he could call me from the jail. When we visited him, we had to leave in the afternoon the day before and get a hotel so we could be there for the allowed visitation hour in the mornings. We visited him at least once a week. I did a lot of driving.

On April 4, we got a court date for Carlos. It was still going to be another week and half more, but it was an important step. I had to gather all the paperwork that the attorney was requesting. I needed a lot of documents and letters from his legal family members. I created a GoFundMe account, but not a lot of people donated. We got more help from family and friends and our life group leaders from church who donated a thousand dollars. We would not have made it without their help.

Adonaldo's fourth birthday was during the time that Carlos was incarcerated, so it was only my parents, Alia, and I celebrating his birthday with him. We didn't even have a full cake because we were running around all the time. But he was happy when we sang him the birthday song.

The attorney had told us that, normally, cases like his are released on bonds of less than $2,000. I prepared myself monetarily with $3,000 just in case, which were all the donations given to us.

Carlos's bond court hearing was on Tuesday, April 16. There were two scenarios that could happen. First scenario is that he would be released on bond. Second scenario is if the judge decided to not release him and deport him, we could still appeal. During that time of waiting for an appeal, he would remain incarcerated.

The court had assigned Carlos the hardest and strictest judge they had. He had such a reputation that all the attorneys and the jailers had nicknamed him "the devil." Our attorney spoke with me before the hearing and said to me that our case was harder because we had to face the hardest judge. I asked her if I could pray for her before she entered the court hearing, and she responded yes. I grabbed her hands, and I prayed out loud for God to direct her words and her thoughts. I told her that God was in control over this and His will was going to be done. There was no doubt in my mind that God would set Carlos free.

My parents, my kids, and I were allowed to go into the court hearing. The judge seemed very strict; he upheld his reputation well. Our attorney, Claudia Hernandez, did an amazing job. The judge turned to look at the ICE agent and asked him where he stood on Carlos's case. The ICE agent looked at all the paperwork and said, "Well it's a fifty-fifty." Let me tell you, the silent few seconds that passed by seemed like an eternity. The judge then said, "I think if we let him out, he will be a flight risk, and we won't see him again." Meaning he will fail to appear in future court hearings. My heart started to race at that point. However, our attorney, Claudia, insisted that Carlos would follow through because he had a family to support and a good job here in the United States. The judge then looked at us and asked our attorney if we were Carlos's family, and she responded that I was his wife and children and other family members. We couldn't speak, so the only thing that I did was just give the judge a smile, although I don't think he saw me.

Our attorney kept on pressing in and said that her law firm would put their reputation on the line for Carlos. The judge sat back on his chair in silence for about ten seconds. In that silence, I asked God to intervene on Carlos's behalf and to change the mind of the judge. Nobody was moving a hair. Even Alia and Adonaldo were not making any noise. It was a very tense moment.

Finally he said, "Fine. $15,000." He then continued to say, "If he can pay for it, which I don't think he can, $15,000. Let's see if he follows through. Court is adjourned." And then he struck the gavel. This is why he had earned his reputation of being called "the devil." We were told it was time to leave the court still without speaking to

Carlos. Other inmates were awaiting their turn for a hearing. We walked out of the courtroom and back into the lobby area.

We waited outside in the lobby for our attorney to explain to us what would happen next. She was crying and apologizing for the judge. I told her not to worry, that she did what she could and that she did great. I asked her if I could pay the $3,000 that I had and get Bernado released and pay the rest later in payments (I know that was a stupid question now that I have been through this). She responded that the $15,000 had to be paid in full in order for him to be released. Typically, the courts give up to thirty days to pay the bond so that the detainee can be released from detention.

Our attorney stated that she was going to ask the court to hold a separate bail hearing to reduce the amount because she and other lawyers believed that the judge was being too hard. Two years later, I don't know if she did or not, but I am guessing she didn't. We were later reassigned to another attorney.

I would be once again indebted to my parents because they lent us the money needed to pay off the full $15,000. We all drove back to Waco that evening. The following morning, I got the check and all the things needed and drove back to Pearsall once again with my kids. We stayed in the hotel that night because we needed to be at the detention center at 9:00 a.m. Otherwise, he would have to wait until the following day to be released. I paid all the money and signed all the paperwork, and they were going to release him around 3:00 p.m. We waited outside in the truck for hours until he was released at eight thirty at night on Wednesday April 17, 2019. I still have the video of when we saw him at a distance walking out of the front door. Adonaldo saw him, and he started running toward him, saying, "Papi, Papi." Alia would just make screaming sounds because she was merely eleven months old.

By then, it was so late, and we were so hungry that we just went to get some burgers and went back to the hotel room. The following morning, we drove to Waco. Friday, April 19, the following day, was my birthday. I did not have any kind of celebration for my birthday. I just wanted to rest. On Sunday the twentieth, we drove back home to Fort Stockton, and Carlos went to work on Monday. God had answered our prayers and had met me at my level of faith.

7
CHAPTER

Dancing with Jesus

On May 7, I was staying at home with my kids like I normally would, watching Christian TV, and I felt God bringing to my memory that Carlos was still waiting on a court date. I was feeling lazy, so I ignored the thought. God once again insisted and said, "Go and check the mail because you will get news about Carlos's court date." At that point, I had learned to trust those thoughts that come out of nowhere, completely unexpected. I walked to the mailbox, and sure enough, I found a letter from the US Department of Justice. Right there, I started to cry and to thank God for that letter. I didn't know what the letter was going to say, but I believed it was going to be his court date. I walked very fast to my RV to open it. At the top are the words: "Notice of Hearing in removal proceedings." When I get very excited like that, I tend to read so fast I skip over a lot of words and look at only the ones I think are the most important. He was to have a *master* hearing before the immigration court on May 19, 2020, in San Antonio, Texas. I got extremely excited, and a little worried, because I thought the hearing was in two weeks. It took me a while to realize that the year of the hearing was in 2020, which was a year later. I was a little disappointed, but I was still happy that he had a date.

Something that worried us was the place of the hearing. There were two possibilities, it could either be held in San Antonio or El Paso. El Paso was closer to us, but it was further away from the attorney, and she charged for that distance of travel. It was 550 miles, and we had to pay, if I remember correctly, two or three dollars a mile plus hotels if she had to spend the night. Carlos was wanting me to change our address to Waco so that it would be guaranteed to be in San Antonio. I told him that I would ask God, and if God told me to change it, then I would change it. But if God didn't say anything, then we would leave it alone. Well, God didn't answer anything, and I didn't change it. To God's glory, we did get the hearing in San Antonio, which we are still waiting until today because it has been rescheduled for 2023.

After that, I didn't know what to do. I didn't know what next big thing I was supposed to have a lot of faith for. So I asked God what He wanted me to do, and I felt Him answer, "Wherever you are all planted, you shall be fruitful." So I took that, and I interpreted it as an I need to start a Bible study. I had a friend that I had met at the Laundromat; her name was Jenny. When you live in an RV, unless you have the big fancy ones, you are probably stuck going to the Laundromats to wash clothes. Well it was there that I met her. The first day I saw her, I knew that God's grace and favor was over her life, and I shared that with her. We started to have a friendship. She said that she wanted to learn more about the Bible. At first, we gathered in the park and let the kids play while we talked about God and the Bible.

I took that and said, "You know what, I am going to make a Bible study group." So I met a few more stay-at-home moms, and I started a Bible study group in my RV. I really enjoyed it. I loved researching the topics and teaching. I would spend hours researching and writing. I have always liked teaching. I believe I do have a calling to teach. I just want to teach people who want to learn and teach subjects that I am passionate about.

It started with just two of us; then, we were three, then four, then I signed up to lead a Bible study group at church, and then we grew to about almost twenty for about a month while the summer life groups were happening. We could no longer fit in the RV of course, so I was having to ask for permission to host the life group in different places. Even in the hot summer days, we would meet in a shaded part of the park in almost one hundred-degree temperature. However, I would see many great things in these meetings. God was definitely growing my spiritual gifts. This is the time I developed my gifting in words of knowledge.

The night of May 30, 2019, I had an important dream. I dreamed that there was a tornado coming toward my RV. I stood in the middle of my home as the tornado was right outside the wall. I stood without any fear, alone, and with much boldness, spoke directly to the storm. I cursed the storm, and I ordered it to go away in Jesus's name. I kept saying the name of Jesus over and over again. Then the tornado left; my house was very much destroyed, but I had won that battle. Then my dream ended. I find it interesting that in those times of spiritual warfare, I am not asking God for help. I already know He is with me, and the power comes from Him. Also during those times, there's no time to think; you must be ready to start fighting.

Two days later, June 1, we were under a tornado warning. I saw in the sky the clouds beginning to circle around as if the tornado was about to form. We had huge hail hitting the top of our RV and strong winds. I am not going to lie. I was a bit scared at that moment. I told Carlos about my dream, and he was thinking that I was making it up. However, even in his unbelief, I stood right in the middle of my RV, just where I was in the dream, and I put my hands up and started to very quietly speak to the storm just like I did in my dream. I did it quietly because I could feel Carlos making fun of me in the back. I knew that he didn't believe me and was almost mocking me, but I did it anyways. The rest of it, I said it internally. In less than two minutes, the formation stopped, the hail stopped, the winds calmed down, and the clouds began to get back to normal. I looked at Carlos and said, "See." He still didn't believe me and said it was all a coincidence. I ignored him, and I thanked God for the dream and for stopping the tornado.

I knew and I felt that God was calling me to a higher level of anointing. I was not able to do all of this before, and the more I witnessed and did, the more I wanted God to keep using me. The summer was over and so was the Bible study. I didn't start another life group because the cold time was coming around, and I don't like the cold weather. When the cold weather hits, I just want to be cooped up in my blanket.

September came around, and at Grace Point church, we started what was called the twenty-one days of prayer. These were prayer meetings leading up to the conference. Every afternoon at six, we would meet for one hour of prayer at the church. I would always start by praising God and thanking Him. Then I would ask God to speak to me in any area that He wanted. I asked Him to tell me something that He wanted others to know of, to show me a vision of what was to come. I wanted to be His instrument no matter what came against me and no matter the consequences.

Then something that I still cannot explain started to happen. I started to feel fire coming down through my arms and into the palm of my hands. I held my hands up, and I felt my hands on fire. It was not just that my hands were warm or that my hands went from cold to hot. I felt a burning sensation as if I had just put fire in the palm of my hands. For three seconds or so, I was getting a little worried, and I was about to call for help. But just when that happened, a peace came over me, and I was filled with such tranquility. When my hands were feeling with fire, I had a sense that God was imparting on me healings. The fire was meant to be used for divine healings. I started to cry at that point because I felt so humbled that God saw my heart, my wants, and my desires. He had placed ministries in me.

Ever since I got saved and felt the presence of the Holy Spirit (or Jesus or God), I would lift my hands to about the height of my chest area. And in my mind, I would say the words, "Let's dance, Jesus." Now, this did not happen every time, but occasionally, I would feel Jesus's embrace, and sometimes I would stand, and I could feel Him dancing with me. My body would move, without me moving it, slowly to the beat of the music. It was only a subtle rocking back and forth, and occasionally, He would slowly turn me. It's difficult to explain. Sometimes I would lock my body so that if it was me doing the movements, I would not move. But if Jesus was dancing with me, my body would still move. This is something very personal between me and God. He knows me, and He knows that I liked to dance before I became a Christian, and it's something that we share because we know each other.

Almost every day, in the twenty-one days of prayer, I received a word, a vision, or a hurting in a body part for someone else. Let me explain this, I would feel pain, or emotions, in my body that did not belong to me. When this happened, it was God telling me that someone close to me or someone I was going to encounter in the next few hours was having a particular pain, and God wanted to heal them. This was information I did not know before God revealed it to me. I loved those twenty-one days of prayer because I really felt a connection with God at another level that I had never experienced before.

I had many very bold moments where I had to stand in faith in what I believed God was telling me. Sometimes that looked completely impossible. One day, as we sat in the church, I looked at a certain young lady, and I felt the need to go over and talk to her. What I did not know at that time was that in her hurting, she was crying out to God, in silence, saying to Him, "God, come close. God, come close. God, come close." I went over to her, and honestly, I didn't know what to say, but I noticed that she was crying. So since God had not told me why I was going over there for, I did the next best thing. I asked her if I could pray for her. She responded with a simple "sure."

I prayed for her even though she wasn't saying much. Then I felt that familiar nudge, the nudge that God was telling me that they wanted a direct answer for a certain question. So I asked her, "What question do you have for God at this moment?" I could tell that she had never been asked this question before. I said, "God knows you have a question for Him, and He wants you to get it out." I was completely walking out in faith with nothing under me other than God's direction.

She said, "All right, I have a question. Why on earth do other warriors in the faith get released from their pain and taken home, while I am left struggling in my pain?" I had walked right into that one, and it was a huge one.

I responded to her, "Well, I don't know the answer, but let me ask God." I closed my eyes and prayed out loud. I don't prefer to pray out loud, but I do it for the benefit of the other person. I asked God the question she gave me, and I waited for His response. He started to put words in my mind, and I would repeat the words that were being said to me in my mind. God had said that He loved her, and she would not go through that forever. He then added the words, "You need to know that you will not die, you will keep living." Words stopped coming into my mind, so I stopped speaking. I opened my eyes, and she was sobbing. I had no idea what God was talking about, but I have come to learn that it's not my job to know. It is only between God and them. As 1 Corinthians 13:9 says, "For we know in part and we prophesy in part." I wish I could know the entire story, but that is something I have learned to let go of.

I had seen her a few times before with a cane and a fracture boot, but I was thinking that she had an injury. It turns out that she had an incurable disease of the brain, and the doctors were only giving her a year to live. A few days later, she gave her testimony, and she mentioned that previously she didn't want anyone to know about her situation. Her health slowly got better; she also got more confidence in herself. She went back to the doctor, and they did an MRI and saw that her disease had lessened. The doctor had said that it was a miracle. She shared the news with us, and we all were very happy for her. I was very happy for her, but I felt a sense of relief more than anything. There was no way I could have known that information; there was no way I could have "predicted" that she would see a miracle in the progression of her disease. I didn't even know she had a disease.

When I ask God questions like that, I have to turn my mind "off" to make sure it is not my thoughts that I am listening to. After I say something as big as that, I am always relieved that it came to pass or it came out to be true because I can now say, "Yes, that was God," but prior to this moment, I am merely walking by faith. I try to be as truthful as I can be and stick to what I am hearing, not adding anything to it, not taking anything out. Maybe one day I will have certainty or confidence to fully say, "Thus says the Lord," but for now, I am taking it one step at a time.

After this, I decided it was time to take this gifting outside of the church walls. My family and I would go out to the park to ride our bikes or walk. Normally, Carlos and Adonaldo would go on their bikes, and I would walk with Alia because she wanted to ride in her little toddler push car stroller. It was a Step 2 push-around buggy. I would take advantage of my walks, and I would ask God to signal to me any person that He wanted to speak to, heal, or just someone that I should just pray for. This was so fun. I got all kinds of practice in words of knowledge.

My first encounter was with a lady in her sixties perhaps. She was sitting on a park bench as I walked in front of her. God signaled her to me, and I hesitated and kept walking. In my head, I said, "Nope, I'm not ready. I don't know what to say. I better not bother the lady." So I kept walking. Yet I still felt God's tug in my chest. My heart started to race. I decided to turn back and had some small talk with her because I still did not have the courage to say anything else. After a few minutes, I finally told her that God had sent me to her. I felt a pain in one of my ankles, and I said, "Do you feel pain in this area of your body?" And I touched that area in my body. I can't remember if it was my right or left ankle. She then said yes, and she went on to tell me how she got injured. I was jumping for joy on the inside. I told her that God wanted to heal her ankle. I squatted down to her ankle, put my hands on her ankle, and started to pray. I didn't really know how to pray in these situations, so I kind of copied what the preachers on television said they did.

Even though my prayer was probably weak and boring, I did feel the fire in my hands. I knew that feeling that fire meant that healing was taking place. I tried to make it quick because I was a little worried other people would see me. I got up, and I asked her to check it. She said it felt a little better. I said, "Let me pray again." This time, I was more confident in my prayer, and when I was praying, I felt the fire in my hands again. I got done praying, and I said, "Check it again." She said that she did not feel any more pain. She could stand on it, and even the swelling went down a little. I saw her again about three weeks later, and she said that she still had no pain in her ankle.

I started to do this almost every time I went to the park. I got more and more confident at walking up to random strangers that God had signaled to me. The majority of the time it was more words of knowledge than healings. God knew the questions in their hearts and minds, so nothing caught Him by surprise. He just needed a willing ear to be able to speak their answers to, which I was willing to be.

I remember a situation that really marked me. A young woman was jogging, and God signaled her to me. She was carrying a heavy burden in her heart because she was a middle school teacher, and one of her students had committed suicide a few weeks back. She was in some way blaming herself for not having done more. God put words in my mouth about how she needed to release herself from that. God spoke such love into her life. She cried, and I cried with her; then, we went on our way. Once the cold time came around, we stopped going to the park.

8

CHAPTER

The Donavyn Chapter

Carlos's work company got bought out by another company called Tierra Lease services. The owners of this company were God-fearing men. They examined the immigration status of all their new employees. The majority had no issues, but others had to renew their work permit or their visas. They gave those a certain amount of time to get their situation in line. They took it upon themselves to pay an immigration attorney to get all the ducks in a row for all the five or so employees that still needed to file some immigration paperwork.

Carlos was a bonded alien, which meant that he was allowed to stay in the United States but had not been given work authorization yet. I called Mr. Tommy, and I asked him if we could continue with our attorney and with the process we had. They got in contact with our attorney and made sure everything was true and in order. After they discovered that it was, they decided that it was best for Carlos to continue with our attorney, and they made a few payments to her office, something that they did not have to do. They did it out of the goodness of their hearts and their generosity.

Immigration processes are not cheap, and they are not quick. Thanks to Carlos's job, our attorney was able to file for Carlos's work permit. About a month later, we got a response that it was approved, and two weeks later, the work permit card came in. The next process has been the longest and the most expensive. Even today, three years later, we are not done paying the attorney, and we still have not had the court hearing.

Months later, we got a notice in the mail for Carlos's biometrics appointment. This was going to be the first time we would go into a government office together. The date of that appointment was December 9, 2019, in El Paso, Texas. Carlos was nervous and so was I. The main reason was because there was an immigration checkpoint on the road from El Paso back to Fort Stockton. We didn't know if they would accept his court release documents. They were supposed to, but we knew that there was a chance that things could go bad if an officer decided not to accept them. We felt that it was somewhat of a risk, but we had to go to his appointment regardless. It was a three-and-a-half-hour drive to El Paso. It was very cold and rainy when we went in to the biometrics appointment, and we were out in less than thirty minutes. On our way back, we discovered that the immigration checkpoint was closed that day. We didn't know if it was always closed or just during the time we passed. Whatever the case, we were very relieved. We knew that God was with us and that He had control over everything. We got back home safe and sound.

During those cold months, I don't like to get out of the house unless I really had to. So I took advantage of that and read books about words of knowledge, prophecy, and healings. I remember reading Shawn Bolz's book *God Secrets: A Life Filled with Words of Knowledge*. I loved that book so much. I also read Mark Batterson's book *Whisper: How to Hear the Voice of God*, which I also loved. I continued to wake up early, and after making lunch for Carlos, I would make myself a cup of coffee and sit to read the Bible and all the other books afterward.

I was thinking that if I was really being used by God in healings, then the next step was to take it to the hospitals or clinics. I really wanted to go in, with permission from the hospital of course, and pray over the sick that were in the hospital. However, Carlos thought that it was a bit much, and he didn't let me. I really desired to go and see if I would see miraculous healings by God through me. Carlos was a believer, but he was not on board with the idea of me going to hospitals. Plus, I had two small children that I had to take care of at home.

For the time being, I decided to give it time and allow God to work in Carlos. I said to God that if I were to do that, He would have to allow Carlos to see that it was not just my emotions but actually Him working through me. Then a program on TV came on about the three heavens. I had left that subject abandoned this entire time; certain sparks like this one would need to pop up for me to continue the wondering of what exactly I experienced. I could never get a clear picture because the preachers that do talk about the different heavens can't agree on where each one is. Therefore, I would always leave it alone.

One day while watching the show *Ancient Aliens* on History channel, something they said captivated my attention. I like to watch that show. I don't believe everything they say, but I do like the series. I was watching season 5, episode 7, titled "Prophets and Prophecies," and toward the end of this episode, they spoke about string theory and Albert Einstein's theory of special relativity. As I was watching this, my heart started to race. Was it a different dimension? Was it a zero-point energy or field? I recorded the show and watched it again. Does science already have a name or a theory to what I witnessed? I can't be certain. I don't know enough about string theory much less zero-point field. So I did what I always would do and left it alone. However, this was something that stayed in the back of my mind.

COVID started to pop up on the news, and for the first time ever, I started to pay attention to politics. Before this year, I could care less about who was president or who was running for a local office. However, this year was a very important year of change for me, and it was to many other Americans as well.

My family and I started to go to a different church, a small Hispanic church in Fort Stockton. The services were on Sunday afternoon, and they were in Spanish. I thought that this would help Carlos keep growing in his spiritual life.

Carlos's job was a financial blessing, and we were very thankful for it. However, I started to notice a change in him. The more I grew in the giftings, the more I would have problems with Carlos. Also, my kids would regularly get sick. I knew where it was coming from, and I prayed against it; however, it wouldn't stop. I would tell Carlos to pray with me so that we could break whatever that was off us. He would never want to. His behavior started to change. He would not want to go to church with us, even if he was not working. He started to drink with his friends, something he had not done in years. Something in him was drastically changing. I blamed it on the devil, and I would pray about it, but our marriage started to crumble. We argued more and more.

When he was released from the detention center, he had a new perspective and was very thankful to God. But as the months passed, he seemed to forget and grew cold. God was answering all my prayers for all his immigration issues, but Carlos's thankfulness started to take a seat in the back. Carlos thought of himself as self-sufficient, and he hardened his heart toward us, his family, and toward God.

Carlos had gotten to the point where he started to get home and get on his phone to play Call of Duty or just be on Facebook. He started to not pay attention to me but would sometimes still play with the kids for about an hour. After a few days, the hour turned into half an hour, then to five minutes with the kids. Then, he didn't play nor speak much with the kids nor myself unless I spoke to him. I didn't know what to do anymore; my marriage was falling apart.

In February of 2020, due to all the problems with Carlos, my blood pressure levels started to rise to dangerous numbers once again. One day, he got home and went straight to his game. I had enough of it, and I told him that he was no longer present with us anymore. That caused an argument, and I felt like I was having a heart attack. I told Carlos how I was feeling, and his response was that I was just exaggerating. I felt like I couldn't breathe. I saw that he did not even bother to get out of bed. I took a seat because I couldn't stand anymore. I called my father in Waco, and I told him how I was feeling. He said that I probably was having some kind of heart failure and that I needed to go to the cardiologist. Well, at that point, I did get Carlos's attention, and he did come and check on me. I started to shake and become really cold. He helped me get a blanket and attended to the kids. I calmed down and was able to get a little sleep that night.

The following morning, everything was covered in snow, and I really did not want to go out in that weather. However, I noticed that my heart started to act just like the night before. I was once again struggling to breathe. I was a little scared at this point. I didn't want to die and leave my kids without their mother, so I prayed for God to protect me, and I asked Carlos to take me to the hospital.

I got checked in, and even though I was not feeling as bad as the previous night, my blood pressure numbers were dangerously high. I was at 190 over 130. I thought it wasn't that big of an issue because in my reasoning, I had felt worse with a flu.

I was in communication with my family, and they were messaging me that I should ask for different tests to be done to me while I was in the hospital. I thought that it was going to drive up the bill, but I decided to go ahead and have them done. In reality, I just felt like going to sleep. They gave me a pill for the blood pressure, and they left me in the room until the test results were in. During that time, I did fall asleep. As the hours progressed, my blood pressure started to come down, and I started to feel better.

It was a reminder for me that God could very well decide to make my second chance a short one. The doctor had said that I was under a lot of stress, anxiety, and perhaps depression. He gave me a few pills while in the hospital and also prescribed me more medication. I was under stress, and I was a bit heartbroken, but I was definitely not accepting the anxiety and depression diagnosis. However, to calm myself down, I took the pills the doctor gave me in the hospital. They released me that same day, and I went home and slept some more. The next day, I took the prescribed anxiety medication, and I really did not like it. I felt like I was a walking zombie high on drugs completely numbed to my feelings. I didn't like that feeling, and I decided I was not going to take those pills. I purposed myself to get better on my own with only God's help. The blood pressure medicine I did continue to take, sort of.

How did I get here? How did things change so quickly? I thought. Once again a roller coaster of highs and lows. Me and Carlos talked after that, and things seemed to calm down for a little while. This experience gave me a reality check. I was too worried about the things in this life. I remembered the words that God had spoken to me while in "second heaven." I realized that I had not done anything with that, other than tell my classes where I taught about my experience. I had the idea of the book, but I have never been a writer. I can't possibly write the book myself. So I started to think of ways that the book could be written without me doing the writing. I felt like Moses when God asked him to go and speak to Pharaoh. Moses replied that he was the wrong guy for the job because he stuttered. I told God that I was the wrong one for the job because writing was not my thing. Regardless, I started to write. I wrote about a chapter and then I abandoned it.

I took everything one day at a time. I prayed, read my Bible every day, and I continued to ask God to keep on using me. At church, we had another fifteen days of prayer happening, and I tried to go to all of them. I loved spending time with God, especially when I got to leave the kids at home and be able to concentrate only on speaking to God.

Monday, March 2, 2020, was just another day of prayer for me. As I drove to the church, I heard all the commotion of the police cars and ambulance happening near a school. I had no idea what was going on; my mind was on getting to the prayer meeting. At the prayer meeting, some of the ladies started talking about how there were too many police cars. I didn't think much of it at that time. Then they switched the conversation to other things. After that, it seemed like gossip to me, so I stopped paying attention to their conversation. We started the prayer and enjoyed my time with God.

The following morning, I was scrolling through my Facebook account, and I saw a lot of "pray for Donavyn" on my feed. I had no idea who this young man was. I continued to scroll down not thinking much about it. Then suddenly, God interrupted my scrolling, and a thought came into my head that said, "He is not going to make it. He will pass away." I sat up so quickly after that and threw my phone to the side of the bed, and I asked God if that thought was from Him. I had a feeling that it was even though I did not get another response.

Me being the person that I am, with many mistakes under my belt, went on Facebook and wrote, "When I hear from God that someone in critical condition isn't going to make it. But everyone is praying for healing, as they should. That's when I REALLY hope it's one of those times that I am wrong." Yep, I know what you are thinking. That was a post I tried to delete after I posted it, but a feeling or a thought would come to my head about leaving it there. I would change the privacy of it and make it to where only I could view it. Then minutes later, I would put it back to friends only. I couldn't bring myself to delete it. From that post, as stupid as it was to post it, two things came from it. One was a brother from church called me because of it and was wanting to go to the hospital to pray for his family. As he was still speaking, God told me to tell him to go. The second thing that came from it was drama. A few of the women that went to church with me commented that God was capable of doing miracles and that all we had to do is pray and have faith that God was going to do a miracle. I simply responded that God could do those things.

That same day in the afternoon, I went to the prayer meeting again. The same women that had commented on my post were there too. I didn't say much. If you know me personally, I am very much an introvert, and I love to keep to myself. I usually don't talk much.

They said that as a group, as a church, we should pray for the young man. I kept my mouth shut and just went along with it. However, something in my spirit just felt uneasy. Meanwhile they were praying out loud, I tuned out their prayer and told God that I wasn't even sure if it was Him speaking to me. I have never heard of anyone alive today prophesying someone's death. I have read in the Bible where the prophet Nathan told David that his son would not live or when Isaiah told king Hezekiah that he would die, or when Peter meets with Ananias and Sapphira. There's more examples like this in the Bible. Despite that, I said to God, "Your will be done, Father." I will either be completely wrong and look like a moron, or I will be right and still look bad. I didn't say anything else that day at church. I felt out of place even though they didn't say anything to me directly.

The following day, I found the mother's profile on Facebook. The first thing I did after sending her a friend request was rush to put that comment in private where only I could see it. Then I got in my room and really sought God's face. I told God that I was willing to stand, alone if I had to, but only if I was certain that what I was saying came from Him. I wanted a confirmation of what He had told me before, and I wanted it right then. God knows I'm persistent at times.

I had a vision at that moment, a vision like I had never seen before. I saw a sun coming up from the horizon. The more the sun rose, the lighter my vision got. I saw a few mountains in the distance. Then I saw Jesus standing next to Donavyn. Their backs were turned toward me. I could tell that I was merely given permission to see some part of this, not all. Jesus was wearing his traditional robe with a shawl over his head and sandals on his feet. I couldn't see what Jesus's face looked like, but I knew that was Him. Then I saw Donavyn standing next to him. I didn't know what Donavyn looked like either since I had never seen him before, yet I knew that it was him. Jesus then puts his right arm over Donavyn's shoulders, kind of as if he was saying to him, "Hey, buddy, come here." Jesus held him closer to his chest. I couldn't see facial emotions, but I could tell that Jesus was not wanting Donavyn to feel any sadness. Neither of them talked; they both just stood there looking forward at the horizon wanting to walk toward it. Then the light started to dim down, and the colors turned into shades of brown. The sun came down, everything turned black, and the vision ended.

This vision lasted probably about five seconds. I immediately knew what it meant. Donavyn was already with Jesus. They couldn't walk to the horizon because he was still being kept alive here on earth, but his spirit was no longer here. This was really hard for me. I had never operated at this level before, with people I had never before seen in my life. I knew that my assignment was to tell the mother of this child. A few hours later, I got the notification that the mother of the child, Jennifer Vaugh, had accepted my friend request. I felt so unprepared for all of this.

I called my pastor at that time, and I wanted to ask him for guidance because I didn't know how to go about it. He was kind enough to listen to me while he was at work. He told me that he didn't believe I was lying, he was believing me, but that I had to really think if I was going to go to the mother. Then he said that if it all went south that the church could look bad too, which I did agree with. Nothing that he said was wrong. He was just airing on the side of caution. He said that even though God had said that to me, that there was still the possibility of God changing His mind. He mentioned a time in the Bible where God changed His mind. He said so if you are going to go through with this, just end on that note, maybe God can change His mind. I agreed with everything my pastor said. It seemed like the safe thing to do. Now I just had to find a way to tell Jennifer, Donavyn's mother.

I still had the women from church posting things on their Facebook contrary to what I was prophesying. All I saw on my Facebook feed was "pray for Donavyn," "Donavyn strong," "God can do miracles," and "Donavyn will come out testifying from this." If I got out of Facebook, all the businesses had on their windows or on their signs "Donavyn strong." I didn't disagree with it. I thought it was a sign that people still believed and that the entire town came together in prayer for this young man. I believe this is what Christians should do in these situations, and I would be the first one in line to pray, had I not gotten the word that Donavyn was not going to return. I was stuck in a really hard place. Carlos at home was saying the same thing as the pastor.

It was here that I learned that the road of a prophet is a very lonely one. I thought that prophecy and all God's gifts were so awesome and cool, and I loved telling people how God was going to heal them, how God would better their lives, or how God would bless them. Until God brought me in deeper and showed me the true walk of the prophet. "Prophecy hurts," I said to God. I felt that I was without a friend in the world. I told my family, and they were just like Carlos and my pastor. All of which I understood. If it I would have been in their shoes, I would have done and said the same thing. I recognize it was a very strong statement to say, and if it didn't come out to be true or if it didn't come to pass, I was going to look like a witch that was used by the devil.

I read an article online, which I shared on Facebook, titled "You Don't Want to Be a Prophet" by Eric Barreto. He said in his article,

> Prophets tend to not have such idyllic hopes for God's call. Prophets know too well that the to call of God to speak hard truths is paved with difficulty. The prophet's road is lonely not because she escapes the hubbub of everyday life in order to retreat and draw near to God. No, the prophet's road is lonely because she is called to the most troubled corners of the world, places which existence we would rather deny or ignore. The prophet's road is lonely because she must speak boldly to an upside-down world that doesn't realize it is upside-down. The prophet sees the world as it really is while we see the prophet and marvel that she is walking on the ceiling.

I continued to say to God that I would do His will no matter what. I reached out to Jennifer that day via Messenger, and I told her that I needed to speak to her because I had a message from God. I was shaking as I sent out this message, and my heart was racing. She responded a few hours later. We exchanged phone numbers, and she said she would let me know when she was available to receive my call.

On Wednesday, March 4, the local news was reporting about Donavyn. I was not aware of his condition; the only thing that I knew is that he collapsed on the track at the middle school. I had read on Facebook that he had asthma, and that is probably what led to his collapse. The news reported:

> A middle school student in Fort Stockton was life-flighted to a Lubbock hospital after collapsing during track practice Monday. According to his Go-Fund-Me page, 8th grader Donavyn Vaughn went into cardiac arrest and both of his lungs collapsed.

That was all the information I had about Donavyn's health condition.

That evening, we received Carlos's work permit card in the mail. We had been waiting for it for weeks, and we were happy it had arrived. I went to church that evening for Wednesday service. While we were in worship, the Holy Spirit told me, "Prepare yourself, she will reach out to you shortly." I looked at my phone and put it on vibrate. Thirty seconds later, I got a message from Jennifer on Messenger saying that I could call her. I prayed for God to direct my words. To be honest, I still did not know how I was going to tell a suffering mother that her child was no longer going to live among us. God was going to have to put words in my mouth.

I went outside the sanctuary to the lobby, and I called her. She put me on speaker with some other family members that were in the room. Even more pressure for me, but I believed I had an assignment to do, so I pressed in to tell her my vision. I said it as calmly and as nicely as I could. After I shared the vision, I said to her, "I believe Donavyn is no longer with us. He has been with Jesus since yesterday." There was a silence for about three seconds from the other side of the line. Then I took the words that my pastor at that time had said to me to ease the news. I shouldn't have said this, but I did. I said to her, "You know but maybe God can change His mind. Maybe God will hear all the prayers from the entire town praying, and maybe His mind can be changed about this matter." I regret having said that. I was giving them false hope. They responded to me that they believed me and believed my words but that they were going to continue believing for a miracle and for God to change His mind. "That was all I wanted to share with you. That is all God has shown me. If you need to call me later or reach out to me on Facebook, you can do that at any time." We said our goodbyes and hung up. The call took about ten minutes, so I walked back into the sanctuary for the remainder of the service.

The following morning, we headed out to Odessa, Texas, to the Social Security office. Since we had received Carlos's work permit in the mail, we knew the next step was to fix his social security. We struggled a lot with his social security because it had a wrong date of birth for Carlos. Before we completely left the RV park, to head to Odessa, God whispered to me, "Take his birth certificate." I stopped and said to Carlos, "We might need the birth certificate." But then I dismissed the thought and said, "Nah, we have other things that have that information." Huge mistake. We drove all the way there, and finally when it was our turn, the first thing they told us was, "We are going to need his birth certificate." Well, we drove back home to get the birth certificate and returned to Odessa, which was a three-hour drive. We walked back into the office with Carlos's birth certificate and got all the issues fixed. When God whispers like that, it's hard to distinguish between my thoughts and His voice. Boy did I screw that one up.

The next few days passed without much change, until Saturday. I was at church in the morning selling menudo that sister Vicky had made. It was delicious by the way. I had arrived late, and the other women had almost sold it all. Since I was at church, I went into the sanctuary to pray. I needed, yet again, another confirmation that I was doing the correct thing. I laid it all before God. God told me that He wanted another sister to join in with me to pray. I knew God was also calling her to walk in the prophetic gifting. We prayed together.

Around noon, completely unexpected, I got a call from Jennifer. She asked me if I had received any other messages from God about Donavyn. I answered her, "No ma'am, not since Tuesday." She then asked me if I could ask God one more time if He was going to change His mind about Donavyn. I said to her that I could ask but that I couldn't guarantee an answer. She said that she would appreciate it if I tried. I told her that I would call her back once I got an answer or once I knew that God wasn't going to answer me.

I got into prayer, and I simply asked God if He was going to change His mind. Almost immediately, I felt a response, and His response was very clear, "I am not changing my mind. Donavyn is already with me." That was it, that was all I got.

All the whispers, sayings, visions that I get are always very short. They last only a few seconds. I took longer to give her a call back than God answering my question. Many thoughts came through my mind at that moment. What if it was not God and it was just my mind? Why am I the only person saying that this young man is not going to make it? Am I even certain that I am listening to God? What if it is evil spirits that I am listening to? On the natural side of things, my thoughts were: What if she calls the cops on me? What if she has someone come and do harm to me or my children? When have I heard any other person, that is way more wise and knowledgeable in the things of God, say what I am saying right now? My head was a mess, but I knew that there was no way around it, and I couldn't cower down now.

I gave her a call about thirty minutes later. I said to her that I did get a response from God. "I don't know how else to say this. There is no nice way to say it, so I am just going to say it as God said it to me. He said that He was not changing His mind and that Donavyn has been with Him for a few days now. I am so sorry." I thought that she was going to cuss me out at the very least. I thought that she was going to take out all her frustrations on me. There was a three-second silence between us. She then took a deep breath and said, "Thank you, I needed that confirmation. I had felt that my baby boy was no longer with us, and I just needed that confirmation." I kept on apologizing because I didn't know what else to say. I said that if she needed anything, she could always message or call me. She thanked me again, and we hung up the call. I felt such a relief after that call.

I was in a group message with some members from church and the pastor, and I decided to message them about what just happened. I thought that they would be just as happy and relieved as I was, but that was not the case. There was a little drama and I decided to withdraw from that church.

That same Saturday in the afternoon, after I stopped messaging the church members, I saw a Facebook video of a pastor that had gone to pray for Donavyn. He was doing a live video from his car, and he was saying that the doctors had told the family that the following day, Sunday, at 5:00 a.m., the doctors were going to check for any kind of brain activity or any kind of life in Donavyn's body, and if they found nothing, they were going to recommend they pull the plugs. I did find out on Thursday that he was being kept alive by machines and that he had no brain activity. However, I did not know that the doctors were already thinking about pulling the plugs.

This pastor went on a live video to ask everyone he knew to pray for Donavyn's recovery. He had just come out from seeing the family and praying for them. He was asking everyone to believe wholeheartedly that God would lift him up. I felt that he had good intentions while filming this video, but he never consulted the Lord before doing this. I watched this video many times, and each time I watched it, I tormented myself with doubt.

I asked God why pastors like this did not ask God what He was going to do. "Have we become so eloquent in the way we petition things from God, but have closed ears to a response from Him?" "Have we become askers and not listeners?" I did not get a response from God, probably rightly so.

I was so nervous and stressed. I needed to constantly calm myself down because my body would get uncontrollably shaky for a few seconds. I told Carlos everything that I had on my mind, and he didn't really know what to say. I said to him that if it was really God speaking to me, then I was now operating at a higher level than I ever was before. I kept on checking my phone all night long for an update. I didn't sleep that night. Once it was 5:00 a.m., I really couldn't sleep because of the anxiety. What could the outcome have been? Did they pull the plugs? Did God listen to all the prayers and changed His mind? I checked all the Facebook pages constantly for news, but nobody was updating. Finally at 6:00 a.m., I couldn't wait anymore, and I decided to message Jennifer and ask her what had occurred. She messaged me back at seven that Donavyn had passed away.

I didn't know how to feel or what emotions I should have. On one hand, I was relieved because this meant that I had passed the assignment God had given me. But on the other hand, Donavyn had passed, and I knew everyone was going to be saddened by this news. My flesh wanted to shove it in every doubter's face that I was right all along. But I didn't. I had to suffer with the ones that suffered and cry with the ones that cried. I decided to go to the other church I used to go to previously that morning. There was a married couple there that believed my words and were a little more supportive than everyone else. I felt a little comfort being around them, but I was still very lonely on that road of the prophet.

9
CHAPTER

Problems with Carlos

Everyone was concerned about the arrival of COVID-19 to our local area. Restrictions were being put in place. They shut down schools for one positive case. We remained at home as much as possible. I used that time to take several online courses like Keith Ferrante's "All Things Prophetic" online course, which I got really behind on very quickly. I also paid for Shawn Bolz's "God Secrets" online course that went along with his book. While I was taking the "All Things Prophetic" online course, we were given homework assignments. I was able to do the first two homework assignments on time. Then I got very busy and couldn't keep up with the class. The first homework assignment was to scroll through my Facebook friends and see who God signaled to me and position myself to receive a word from the Lord for them. I did this with three of my Facebook friends. It was meant to be a simple prophetic word for them, but God was giving me words of knowledge for them. That was fun. I got visions and thoughts of which all came out to be true. Then a few days later, our homework assignment was to do a live video and try to prophesy on the spot. I had to send the kids away with their dad so that I could concentrate on this assignment. I was only planning to do a live broadcast for about ten minutes, but it turned out to be a full hour. I sat in front of the screen with my guitar playing and singing a Christian song. Someone would come on, and as I was singing, I would ask God to reveal something to me about them. It was amazing. I loved it. I got to say something to at least ten people. It sounds like few people, but to me, it was a lot.

88

I loved doing that, but I had some people that didn't like it, and they said that it seemed like I had a 1-800 direct line to God. I think they meant in as an insult, but I thought that their insult was a complement. Regardless, I stopped doing the lives. I am very much an introvert, and I only did that for the assignment. I was proud of myself for doing it. But as usual, after every high, there is low on the way. I had done the Lord's will, and the devil knew it and knew exactly where to hit me—Carlos.

The oil industry took a hard hit those months, and Carlos's hours started to get cut. He was staying home more than going to work. We had started to argue once again. He was repeating the same patterns as last time. One day, he got home late from work, and we started to argue; we raised our voices, and he cussed at me, something that he had not done before. I was having a bad day, and I wasn't having it. At that moment, I really wanted to leave with my children. God responded in that second that I was thinking that. He said that I had the green light to leave. I couldn't believe He gave me permission to leave.

I was shocked that He gave me permission because four years prior, Carlos and I had an argument, and I packed my things to leave with my baby, and on the way to my parents' house, God told me that I had to go back to my husband, so I did.

This time, I packed the majority of my things, which were almost all clothes, and I packed the kids' clothes. I put everything in the truck. Carlos was lying in bed trying to stay out of my way, which made me even more mad that he wasn't trying to stop me. I got my two children and put them in their car seats and our dog and drove off headed to Waco. It was almost nine o'clock at night when I left Fort Stockton. I was headed to my parents' house, which was seven hours away. I was going to drive all night long.

I had sold my car two months prior to this to pay for immigration charges. So we were down to just Carlos's truck, and that is the vehicle I left on. Carlos stayed behind without a vehicle. As soon as I drove off, I told God that I wanted Him to sit in my passenger seat, to keep me company, the entire way there. I also told Him to not tell me to go back to my husband because, this time, I was not going back. I told him that even if I did go back with him at a later date, I was not going back then. I knew God was listening, and He sent angels to sit with me and accompany me. I felt them. I drove about two hours, and there was a tornado warning in that area. It was almost midnight, and I only had $50 with me, which was only enough for the gasoline to get me to Waco. I was thankful that my children fell asleep very quickly because I didn't have money to buy them food or snacks along the way.

When I came to the area where the tornado could hit, it was in the middle of nowhere; it was dark, and there were no cars passing by. I told Jesus that He needed to help me drive during this. I drove very slowly, and there were branches and debris flying in front of me. I checked my phone, and there was a message from Carlos telling me that there was a tornado warning in that area. I didn't answer him, and I even put his messages on ignore. *Now he is worried about us*, I thought. But I wasn't about to start conversing with him; that was the last thing I wanted to do.

Finally, I got past the storm, and there were two things that worried me then. One was that the city could have a curfew in place and no cars could be circulating, and I would have to stop in a hotel. Since I didn't have money for the hotel, I would have to sleep in the truck. The second worry was getting sleepy at the wheel.

I got to the town, and I did not see a single vehicle or police car. It seemed like a ghost town. I was so thankful. Now I just had to stay awake until I arrived at my parents' house. Around two in the morning, my eyes started to get heavy. I still had another two hours to go, so I asked God to help me stay awake. My parents were messaging me to ask me how I was doing and where I was at.

The kids remained asleep, and the road was almost empty. I used this time to talk to God, destress, and try to stay awake. He was just listening to all my burdens, as if He knew that I just needed someone to listen to me. I am almost certain it was Jesus in my passenger seat. At times, I would turn to the seat as if it was a person. I know that sounds crazy, but at that moment, it was so peaceful to know that He was there with me. I didn't care what tomorrow brought because God was with me in that moment. I finally arrived at my parents' house at four in the morning. I thanked God as soon as I pulled up the driveway for sitting in the truck with me. My parents were still awake, waiting on me. I was tired, and so were they, so we all went to sleep.

The next two days passed rather quickly. I still wasn't talking to Carlos. I answered one of his messages saying that we had arrived, and that was all. I was prepared to leave Carlos if it came to it, but I was not conducting myself as if I was single. I stayed at home almost all day except to go get some pizza or burgers for the kids and myself. It was COVID season after all.

That second night at my parents' house, I was in between asleep and awake, and I am not certain if I had a dream or a vision. But I dreamed that I was sitting on a park bench in front of a river or a small body of water during the night. It almost didn't feel like a dream nor a vision; it felt real. I was sitting at the bench watching the stars and the moon. Sitting beside me was God. He was fluffy like a teddy bear but strong and muscular. He was wearing a black leather jacket. I never looked down, so I don't know what kind of pants or shoes He was wearing. I laid my head on his shoulder and put my arm around his arm. He was big and tall. There was plenty of "cushioning" to Him; I didn't feel bones.

We both were silent, listening to the sound of the night and looking at the stars and the moon. At times, I looked at the water to see the reflection of the sky. It had a lovely nature smell, and the air was so pure. There were no other people there, just me and Him. This vision or dream or whatever it was lasted for about one or two minutes. I felt a loving God that was present in the now and that comforted me when I needed it the most.

The following morning as we were praying for our food, I had a small vision. I saw some image that resembled an X or a weird-shaped cross, and then the X started to rotate. As it rotated, the background color turned into a lighter shade. I knew that was God telling me that He was going to turn things around in reference to my relationship with Carlos. I had a feeling that this meant that we were to get back together. I believed it, but I did not act on it. I still was not talking to Carlos, but I would video call him at night so he could talk to the kids. As soon as he answered the video call, I would hand the phone to Adonaldo. Alia only spoke a few words, but she attempted to talk to her dad. Once they were done talking, I would hang up. I was not ready to have that conversation just yet with Carlos, even though I knew it was coming.

The following day, I got sick, really sick. I believed I had COVID. I had diarrhea, a lot of vomiting, shills, weakness, shortness of breath, and the list continues. I just didn't have a fever. During those days, if you didn't have a fever, you could not get tested for COVID. I was really sick for about four days; then, I started to get better. During that time, everyone was worried about me, including Carlos. He video called me, and I decided to answer. I guess word got around that I was really sick. He asked me how I was doing, and I said I was getting better. We didn't speak much, and then I handed the phone to my kids. After I got better, around two weeks after I had left Fort Stockton, Carlos went to my parents' house with my sister and my brother-in-law. I was still not wanting to get back together yet; we still had not spoken or talked about how to solve our issues. He was there for the weekend and had to go back for work.

I had the promise from God that He would turn things around, but I had not seen anything yet. Sunday they were going to leave back to Fort Stockton, and he was expecting me to leave with him. We had barely talked to each other, and when we finally had the conversation, it was a miserable conversation with a little more arguing. So I did not leave with him. The main reason was because I had a cardiologist appointment the following week. The cardiologist was going to run some tests on my heart. I was not missing that appointment. So he went back by himself, but at least we said that we would work on our relationship.

What astonishes me the most is that God showed me that He was still with me despite the brokenness I was going through. Religiosity would say that God had departed Himself from me because I had left home. However, the opposite was true. I continued to have dreams, not just any dreams but prophetic dreams. One night at three in the morning, I heard a loud storm. I checked my phone, and it turned out we were under a tornado warning. After the storm calmed down, I went back to sleep.

I had a dream that I was prophesying and talking to people. Then I had a supernatural knowledge that something was coming. Then I started to see that what I sensed was coming started to materialize. I flew up in the sky, about 200 feet above the ground, and I watched down to see why I was sensing that something was coming. I looked at the waters, and a beast rose from the water in a whirlpool. It rose to attack me and destroy everything and everyone on its path. It was a female beast. When she came out of the water and onto land, she would crawl because she had no legs. However, she moved quite fast. I would rebuke her from the sky, but I couldn't stop her. I would at times slow her down, but that was all I could do to her. I fought her in the spirit for a long time, but I could not beat her. No one else was helping me. I thought that I would be in this battle forever, without her winning or me winning. Suddenly, I felt the support of Jesus behind me. I could not turn around to see Him, but I knew it was Him. The beast saw Jesus and left but was not defeated. She returned to the waters where she had come out from. The dream was more detailed, but this is what I wrote down afterward. As I had mentioned earlier, dream interpretation is not my strong gift. I thought of different things that this dream could signify. But once again, I did what I always do when I can't decipher something, and that is to leave it alone. I figured that in due time, I would know.

Well, the oil field industry kept on going down and down. So much so that the company had to let go of almost 80 percent of its employees. Carlos and my brother-in-law were included among those. One week after Carlos had come to visit us, they were let go from their jobs. They packed all their belongings and drove back with the RVs.

10
CHAPTER

Prophecy Came True

Life went about normal the following weeks. Carlos was still receiving a smaller check from his company because the government had given relief funding to the oil industry. For the time being, we were okay. Carlos and I decided to work on our marriage for our kids and to remain a family. We went to live in an RV park close to my parents' house. It was a fun RV park in Elm Mott, Texas, with lots of things to do and a pool.

Two weeks after we moved there, Alia got very sick. She had been sick for a few days with flu symptoms. She had been running a fever that wouldn't stop. I tried medicine, I tried giving her baths and making her drink plenty of fluids, but nothing would help. I was beginning to ponder if I should take her to the hospital. As she was lying with me on my bed, I was trying to get her to go to sleep because I could tell she was feeling miserable. A few minutes later, I was feeling that the bottom of her feet were getting hot, meaning her fever had gone up. Then something I still cannot explain happened. She raised her head as if she was seeing an angel standing close to the door. Whomever she was looking at was making her smile and giggle. She then said "bye" and waved goodbye with her hand. She waited about two seconds as if the angel had responded bye to her. She said "bye" and waved a second time. I turned in that direction to see if maybe I could see an angel or Jesus, but I saw nothing. She then put her head down and got her head comfortably on the pillow. She closed her eyes and went into a deep sleep within ten seconds. About a minute later, I checked her feet, and they were at normal

94

temperature. That little visit from "someone" completely broke her fever. Her temperature was down to 98.6 degrees, and it stayed down without me giving her medicine after that.

Weeks passed, and I thought it was time for me to go back to school. I went back to school to get an IT degree. It was challenging to say the least. It was all online, and I had to watch the kids as I was in class for hours. I was way over my head. Going to school as an adult is not the same thing as when you are fresh out of high school. I stuck with it, but I was always far behind, and I couldn't pass my certification exams. I thought about quitting many times, but it was too much money to let it all go down the drain.

In late May of 2020, we drove by a lot of land for sale that my parents had been looking at for years. My father really wanted to buy it, but according to my mother, it was too expensive. To be honest, it was too expensive, but the price always kept going up instead of down. Our entire family had gathered together in Waco one weekend, and we all went to go see it. My dad was convinced that he wanted the land. It was in a pretty place out in the country area but not too far away from the city. One of those times that we drove to the land to look at it, I was holding Alia in my arms because she was asleep. I turned down to see her, and as I lifted my head, I smelled a familiar smell from when I was a child and lived in the mountains in Mexico. Almost immediately after that smell, I heard God tell me, "Don't worry, this land will be y'alls." It was too early to say anything at that time because my family members were going to say that I was crazy. We had not even talked to the land owner yet. So I kept it to myself for the time being.

The next week, we got to work on contacting the seller. We got in touch with the realtor. The realtor told us that a company was trying to buy it but that if the deal did not go through that he would give us a call. I was glad at that point that I had not mentioned anything about my "word from the Lord" to my family, and I was definitely not going to share it now. My parents kept on shopping around, looking at other lots and houses. They found a house for sale very close to where they lived. It was a very gorgeous property. They thought that this house was their answered prayer. Everyone in the family liked this house. However, I still had that word in the back of my mind not letting me fully like it. They placed a bid on it, and the owner came back and said that he had many offers, and he would sell it to the one that offered the most money for it. Well someone offered more money, and my parents lost that house. Then another house came along and another, but something would always happen that the offers would not go through or someone would come by offering more. At this point, I really felt the tug from God to press for the land. I would call the real estate agent, and he kept on telling me that nothing had changed and the company was doing some surveying, and it was taking them a while to get back to the bargaining table. So in between me and my sister Lilia, we spoke to the owner of the land and not the real estate agent. He said that there was no such offer from a company and that if we still wanted to buy the land that he would sell it to them that day. We were shocked and glad. I then was confident enough to share the word from the Lord that I had received weeks prior. But we were very excited to be buying the land. About three weeks later, the deal was made.

Carlos found himself a job for the time being although he really wanted to start his own business. I also went back to work. I was a substitute teacher at a few different school districts in the area. Everything was going good. Things were on the up and up.

During the month of October was when the Trump rallies and Trump trains happened all across the United States. For the first time in my life, I was involved in politics. I never used to care about politics, but this year was different than all the other years. I went to a few Trump trains in the Central Texas area. I bought myself a few flags to put in the back of my truck during the Trump trains. I started with two flags, a USA flag (thanks to Russell Walizer Jr. and his business Walizer's flags) and a Trump flag, which was also gifted to me. The first Trump train I went to was in Waco; there were a lot of vehicles. I went with my kids, and we all thought it was really fun. There was going to be another one the following month. But I couldn't wait that long.

I was invited to the Bryan/College Station Trump train the following weekend. Carlos joined us that time. By then, I had bought two more flags. One was a Texas flag, and the other one was a "Jesus is my savior, Trump is my president" flag. I got some pictures and videos of that parade, and I posted them on Facebook. Within a day or two, I started getting a lot of new friend requests, and my videos started getting twenty thousand views or more. That doesn't sound like much, but my videos previously would get one hundred views at most. So that was a big change. The reason my page got so much traffic was because I am Mexican and I am supporting a Republican candidate.

I bought myself my fifth and final flag—the Mexican flag. I had five flags in the back of my truck. Flying high were the Texas and the USA flag, and a little lower were the Trump, Jesus, and Mexico flag. After I put the Mexican flag on my truck, I would get a lot of people cheering me when I would pass by because of the flag. Carlos was not too into it at first, but after he saw how many vehicles there were and how many of those had the Mexican flag, he got a little more into it. We all had so much fun and wanted to go to the next one.

Because I got a lot of traffic on my Facebook, we were then invited to join the Magnolia Trump Train in Magnolia, Texas. That was a little further, but I didn't care; they were fun, and I loved the atmosphere. I would record video on my phone and then go back home and edit the video. These videos would once again get more than ten thousand views. I am a nobody. I am not famous, so I was shocked when I saw those numbers.

My page grew and grew. Until I was, like many other Trump supporters, silenced, shadow banned, or placed in Facebook jail (as we call it). We all know too well that Facebook silences conservative voices. And if it is a little person, like myself, we get squashed really easily. We had prophecies that said that Trump would win, and I believe them. The November elections came, and we all know what happened. I truly believe Trump won. But I'll leave that for another time.

However, God was not done with me yet. I started as a substitute teacher at a local high school. By Thanksgiving, I got offered a long-term substitute position. By Christmastime, I got offered a teaching position teaching Spanish classes. Carlos had now started his own remodeling company. Everything seemed to be going well.

But the reason why I left teaching soon came back to haunt me. I loved my job, and I loved working with the kids. I planned on working there for many years to come, or so I thought. I started my year as I always did. I would tell them a little about myself and my "visit to second heaven." I realized that it was starting to not be as fresh in my memory as before. After all, I had not told my story to anyone in about two years. Sadly, I was starting to forget it.

I was still doing my IT schoolwork after my teaching job. It was hard, especially with two little ones at the house. I would ask God to use me powerfully as He pleased. Well, there were those two or three times that He did. I prayed for a student of mine, Marylin, privately during one of my conference periods, and she received immediate healing. That situation had a good outcome because her parents were believers. The other time had a different outcome, and I got written up.

The start of the following school year, I told my story, but this time, I added Donavyn's story. The kids were left speechless and quiet when I asked if anyone had any questions. I had created a PowerPoint with pictures of everything I was saying, which made everything even more real. This was the only time I would say anything regarding God in front of the entire class. It was a way for me to explain to the kids who I was. I did not get another write up for that, but the principal wrote that I was "pushing the line," which I agree with because it is a secular school after all.

During the first week of school, a young woman was seriously ill in the hospital. She was the daughter of one of the teachers at the high school. They were very loved by the community and had been there for many years. They really are great people with kind hearts. I was the weird new outsider. Once their daughter got sick, everyone was praying for her healing. I had an uneasy spirit when I heard this. I kind of sensed what was to come, but I was not certain about it. I would ask God what He was going to do, but for three days, He did not respond to me. On the fourth day, I was at school, and I received my answer while I was in class. The answer was that she was not going to make it.

When I received this answer, I was not in prayer. I certainly was not wanting to get an answer at that time; it just came to me. I was with a group of kids that I had the previous year, so I knew them, and they knew me. As soon as I got this answer, I went to the back of the room, and I wanted to cry. One of my students asked me if I was okay. I should have just said, "Yes, I'm okay," and left it alone. Any wiser person would have shut their mouths, but since the student and I had a good relationship, I answered him. I said, "I believe God just told me that the young woman is not going to make it. But I hope I am wrong. I really hope I am wrong." Others were listening in, and they asked me to repeat myself. Again, someone wiser would have said, "Never mind, I didn't say anything," but I didn't, and I repeated what I had said. Then, the bell rang, and I said, "But please don't say anything to the teacher or to anyone please. I am not certain of this," thinking that I would gather some courage to go tell the father after school.

Well, the following period, I stood outside the door to greet all the kids coming in, as I always did. I looked to my side, and I saw both principals standing in the hallway, and they seemed mad. I felt something was headed my direction.

I told God that I would leave everything in His hands no matter what came my way. When school was released for the day, the assistant principal came very nicely and said that they needed to speak with me. I could feel fire within me; something was very wrong. I went in to the office, and I said, "Lay it on me."

The principal said, "You are under administrative leave until we do an investigation." I asked him why, and he said that it was because of what I said about the young lady. "Yeah, I can't defend that," he said. I wanted to ask him why he felt like he needed to defend it, but I didn't push it, and I simply said okay. I could see it in his face; there was no changing his mind. I asked if they needed me to leave work for the kids or if they needed me to do anything else to prepare for my absence. The principal responded, "No, we don't need anything. Also, you can't come anywhere near the school or to any after-school events or anything. I want you gone." I find it interesting that he thought I was such a threat to the kids that he wanted me gone, but he waited until the end of the day to tell me.

I just had one thing in mind at that point, I needed to tell the teacher. I wanted it to come from me directly and not from someone else that could perhaps twist my words. "Can I go talk to him so that he hears it directly from me?" I asked the principal.

"Absolutely not," he answered me. "Look, I commend you for what you do, but…" The rest of his words in this sentence are a blur in my memory. "But we will call you as soon as we get done with the investigation," he said.

"All right, I will wait for your call then," I said. I was not hiding, I was not ashamed, I was not apologizing. I still wanted to keep my job, but I was not going to beg for it nor was I going to back down from what I believed God had said. That to me would be to fear man when I have God on my side.

I went home and told everything to Carlos. He was angry. "Why did you say it in front of the kids? Why do you keep getting yourself in these situations?" he asked me.

"I don't know, I don't know," I said. "Are you even certain of what you said?" he asked me.

"No," I responded. I didn't want to lose my job. I loved my job, and I loved my students. However, the thought of me not teaching anymore was not a bad idea. I was not feeling guilty nor worried. I walked outside and called a friend of mine, Marcela. We spoke, and I shared with her that I felt both relieved and worried. She advised me to seek the Lord and to ask Him to show me the way I should go, and she then prayed for me before ending the call.

The following day, I went to the *Jesus hour* at church. I went to church because I needed to pray and lay it all before God. I asked for God's intervention. I said to God that what I wanted most was for His will to be done in my life over anything that I wanted or thought that I needed. To be truthful, I didn't know what I wanted. Part of me wanted to go back to the classroom, part of me didn't. During those two hours, I told God that I wanted to know that day if they were going to fire me or not. Like I mentioned before, patience is not one of my virtues. God knows it too. I asked Him, and about ten minutes later, I received a text message from the principal's phone to go to the school.

I kind of knew what the outcome was going to be, but I was still hoping that they would tell me that I had my job back. They did a "full investigation" in a short amount of time, which meant that their minds were already made up. I walked in, and they said that they had found "other things" (which they didn't tell me what they were) and that they would accept my resignation until four of that same day or that they would take it to the superintendent and it would go on my record. Nothing that I could have said would have changed their minds, so I told them that I would e-mail my resignation as soon as I got out of there. I did not apologize, and I did not walk out of there with my head down.

I saw the father of the young lady there as I was walking out, and now having realized that I was fired anyway, I wanted to speak to him, but I saw his face and his emotional state, and I knew he was not ready for what I had to say. Plus, I was being escorted out by the assistant principal.

Despite how everything occurred, I wrestled not against flesh and blood, and they were not my enemies. They were either being used by the devil or being used by God for a purpose that I did not know about yet. So I left peacefully and without a fight. I said to God that if He wanted to take revenge that I left it up to Him.

I went back home, and I told Carlos that they had fired me. He took it better than the day before; he also felt it was coming. He had said to me that he had prayed to God to save the young woman just so I could be proven wrong. I knew he was frustrated, so I didn't respond.

The following day, I went back to the Jesus hour. I had to assimilate my new reality. I asked God to place a new path before me and to make the light very bright so that I wouldn't take the wrong path. I was in the prayer room for about two hours or more. I had a lot on my mind, and I could only entrust it to one person that was my best friend—God. "I just have one question," I asked God. "Can you show me the young lady?" I wanted to see a vision like I did the last time so that I could then tell the parents. But I did not get a vision.

Immediately, I started to feel in my body what the young lady was experiencing in her body. I felt her breathing. I could feel her lungs and her chest. My eyes were closed, so I was not seeing anything; it was all a physical feeling. For every two or three breaths I took, she took one. It was very agonizing for her, but she was not conscious of it. "Why do you let her keep suffering?" I asked God. "Why haven't you taken her already?" I believe God answered me, "For love" or "Out of love."

I couldn't take it anymore, and I asked God to stop showing me. I wasn't too certain if the response I got was God or my head. I had a sense it was a love for her father, but I couldn't understand it. To this day, I still don't fully understand it. Maybe the parents had to get to a point where they said it's better to end her suffering. I don't know, maybe one day I will know.

Just like Donavyn's passing, the entire town was praying for her recovery as well. It was such a hard time for everyone and for me. I didn't see a lot of drama directed toward me this time, but I am almost certain that everyone was speaking behind my back. There were some teachers and coworkers that I considered friends that stopped speaking to me because of this.

I went to the prayer room for the third day, and I encountered two young men that I had seen before, and I knew they were filled with the Holy Spirit. I went up to them and talked to them about my situation. One of them said to me that maybe God was telling me that the young lady was going to pass because He saw a friend in me and wanted someone to share His secret with. Although that sounds very lovely and I am extremely humbled if it is the case, something about that didn't fit with me. It sounded to me like if God was weak or not capable of handling it on His own. I liked his words, but it didn't sit well with me. Then I told them about Donavyn. I asked them what they would've done if they were in my shoes. They said they would not have shared it with the mother and they would have waited until the person passed to say something. He said that if it was someone he knew, and they knew the Lord, that he would share; otherwise, he would not have the courage to say "thus saith the Lord." I thanked them for their time, and they prayed for me.

I went home, and I messaged Jennifer. I asked her if it would have made a difference if I would have spoken after the fact or when I did. She said definitely when I did and that if I would have spoken after Donavyn's passing that she would not have believed me.

I finally realized something that I felt in my gut but I would never say out loud. I believe that prophecy has become feel-good predictions for people. I was thinking I was doing it wrong, but when I went to the scriptures and I saw what the prophets did and said, it was not always good news, it was not always positive, and it was not always how God was going to bless people.

When I took the online course of "All Things Prophetic," I watched someone say that they had a warning from God, and they wanted to share it; the teacher immediately shut that down. Prophesy is meant to edify the body of Christ, but when I go to scriptures, 1 Corinthians 14:3 says, "But he that prophesieth speaketh unto men to edification, and exhortation, and comfort." Either I was wrong or everyone else was not wanting to take the risks or were not as bold to speak what God had said. "Which one is it?" I asked God. However, He did not respond, so I left it alone.

Since I no longer had a job, I needed to look for one. I started looking for work outside of the public school system. I wanted to put my IT degree to use. I applied at several places for IT-related jobs. I talked to my IT school about getting a job and taking a refresher course. While I waited to hear back from them, I went back to one of the schools I had substituted before. I asked the lady in charge if they were still hiring substitutes, and she responded that they were always hiring subs. So I asked to be placed back on the substitute call list.

Three days after being asked to resign, I walked back into a school to substitute teach. My thought was that it was temporary until I found a new job. The majority of the IT jobs were remote, or work from home, and I didn't have Internet at home at that time. I applied to work at Antioch and was really hoping I would get a job at the church, but once again, I did not get hired. A strong option that I had was to work for a company interpreting for medical facilities remotely. There were many options out there for me. I didn't know which route to take. So to make sure I took the right one, the first thing I did was tell God to show me the way.

Then what I had prophesied came true. Three days after I prophesied her death and two days after I was asked to resign, the young lady passed away. I had the same feeling as when Donavyn passed. Once again, I was relieved that I was hearing God but saddened by the death.

I went back to the school the following week to pick up my things and return the keys. I greeted and talked to the principal, as I used to do every day that I worked there. He was not my enemy. He asked me what I was going to do. I answered that I didn't know. "I'll probably get one of those IT jobs, but I really don't know what God wants me to do now." I said goodbye to him, and I said, "Pray for me," as I was leaving. He said he would. I wanted to close that chapter in my life without any drama. Part of me still hoped they would reconsider, but I knew that it was not going to happen.

I was working as a substitute teacher while I was doing interviews with other companies. One of the interpreting jobs I interviewed for paid $15 an hour. Other IT-related jobs paid $14 per hour. Substituting paid $13 an hour. Then, at the same school I was substitute teaching, I got offered a full-time position for $16 an hour as the "quarantined teacher" as I called it. I took it. I was now making $3 more an hour than as a substitute. I was still looking at other job options, but just like the houses that my parents were looking at, everything seemed to fall apart. For the interpreting job, I didn't have enough Internet at home. The IT jobs were in the afternoon shift, and I needed a quiet office to work at. All of which I didn't have. So I discarded those jobs. There was still one job I was waiting on, and it didn't require Internet. I had applied at the Texas Department of Criminal Justice. If I was to make the change out of the public school system, this was my chance. I got a date set for my first interview the following week.

During the time I was the "quarantined teacher," I had to be in front of the computer all day monitoring when students came into the Zoom meeting. Since I had the time, I started to write this book. I used all my free time to write. Before I knew it, I had finished my second chapter. Could this be why everything happened? Is this the reason I had to be let go of my other job? I asked God to once again open doors if it was His will for my life or close them if they were not what He wanted for me.

One day before I was to have my interview with the Texas Department of Criminal Justice, the principal came to me and said that another position had just opened up that paid forty-four cents more than what I was getting paid. It turned out that one of the teachers had quit that day. I was torn on what to do. I turned to Carlos and my family, and they advised me to take this job that the school was offering. So I did.

When it came time to fill out paperwork, I realized that it was a paraprofessional job. I was going to be making less money than I did as a teacher. I almost wanted to go begging the previous school to take me back. I felt like I was drowning in a glass of water. I was only looking at the difference in the money. One day I actually did call the principal, but he did not answer nor call me back. I would look at scripture, and I saw time and time again what happened to the people that were closest to God. The people that God used the most were not always on the up and up. The more God used them, the more they had trials and persecution. I also thought about working at a Christian school. I had even requested an application and had filled it out, but I could never bring myself to take the application. Something just didn't feel like that was what I was supposed to do.

As I would take my long walks outside, I would ask God to help me overcome this feeling of defeat. The only reason I believe God had sent me here was because He knew that in this job, I would have the time to sit and write my book. God showed me that He was blessing me here by placing me in higher positions in less than two months. Yes, it is less money, but to be quite honest, I liked this job more. I don't have to do lesson plans, I don't have to put in grades, I did have to call parents, but that was only on a rare instance, and I am in a computer lab. I am not up in the front teaching a class. I am simply monitoring the kids, which gave me time to write this book. If I would have continued teaching, at any school, I would not have had the time to write.

I remembered the visions I had of me on a plane traveling to different cities teaching about things pertaining to God. I wonder if I am the only one that God communicates to in this matter. Or am I the only one that is brave enough to say it? I am nobody special for God to use me in this matter. I get very frustrated with my kids all the time. I have little patience. Yes, I see God as my best friend with superpowers, and I tell Him everything. I really don't know where this boldness to speak comes from because in real life, I am very much an introvert. Every hour of the day, I have this sense that God sees everything I do and say. This does not mean that I don't commit mistakes, of course I do, and plenty of them. Could the level of our faith determine the amount God uses us? Or did God place the "measure of faith" in us so that we may then do His work?

I was trying to provide an explanation to what I witnessed, but the truth is that I don't have an explanation. I watched a *Sid Roth's It's Supernatural* video one day, and this one really caught my attention. Sid Roth was interviewing Jim Woodford in his show. Jim is very well-spoken, unlike me. I would like to use Jim's words because they sound so much better than my own. "You have to suspend all that you have been taught about physics, and gravity, and time, and linear space, and special references, they simply do not exist in heaven." He is right. I wanted to try to explain with fancy scientific words what I witnessed, but to be honest, I wouldn't have a clue as to what those words would be. So I'll let the readers decide for themselves.

After finishing this book, I still didn't know what I was going to title it. *My Trip to Second Heaven, My Out-of-Body Experience, My Weird Prophetic Moments*, these were the titles I was contemplating. But neither felt like the right one. I asked God to help me come up with a title. Reading my normal five chapters a day of the Bible, I came across Deuteronomy chapter 11. God is telling the Hebrew people to love and obey all his commandments, and it would go well for them (paraphrased). Then I read verse 21:

> "That your days and the days of your chil-
> dren may be multiplied in the land of which the

LORD swore to your fathers to give them, like
the days of the heavens above the earth."

The words "like the days of the heavens above the earth" jumped at me. *That's it!* I thought. That corresponds with what I witnessed in reference to the location. The version I was reading was in Spanish, and in my Bible, *heavens* is plural. In English, some versions have it singular, others plural. I personally believe it is *heavens*, plural. It signifies, for me, the nearness of God to us His creation. This means that He is close enough to us so that we may hear when He speaks. The heavens are close to us just above the earth. I decided to make *Like the Days of the Heavens Above the Earth* my title.

I keep telling God that I am unworthy of this task and that I'm not a writer. But just as Moses did, I will trust God, and I will go anywhere He leads me. I will trust His plan for my life. He will show me the way.

I would like to borrow these words from Jessica Lynn Jacquez:

> "I finally realized that I didn't need to be ashamed of who I was or what I had been through. Instead, I needed to share my story because I knew it had the power to lighten the burden of shame for others and make them feel less isolated in their struggles. This is #WhyIPublish."

For anyone out there like myself, I wrote this book for you. I want to encourage you to keep on obeying the voice of the Lord. If God wants to use you like He has used me, I want to let you know that it will not be easy; you will have many things come against you, but you will be in the palm of His hand as his precious instrument. If we all would listen to God and be His willing instruments, maybe then it will be like the days of the *heavens* above the *earth*.

ABOUT THE AUTHOR

Aide Parra was born in 1985 in Watsonville, California, but grew up in Mexico and Texas. Aide considers her faith and family to be most important to her. She is a mother of two children and currently lives in Texas.

Aide had a near-death experience in 2015 followed by several powerful prophetic moments throughout the years. She decided to share her story after she realized that her experiences had the power to lift the burden of shame for others and make them feel less isolated in their struggles.